FEATHERS
IN THE
WIND

FEATHERS
IN THE
WIND

The Boobies and Gannets of the Americas

A Cancer Doctor Discovers Birding
and Rediscovers Himself

by EDWARD ARENSON MD

FEATHERS IN THE WIND

Published by Compass Rose Publishing
228 Park Ave. S #620056 New York, NY. 10003-1502

Printed in the United States of America

Hardcover ISBN# 979-8-9941958-0-2
Softcover ISBN# 979-8-9941958-1-9

All illustrations and photos by the author except as noted and
credited in the captions.

Cover and Interior Design by Madeline Mafilios and Thomas Hurd.

First Edition

I wish to dedicate Feathers in the Wind to my three wives—Irene (first), Julianne(second), and Aura, all of whom have demonstrated exceptional patience and tolerance for me and my birding passion. Collectively, I have spent fifty-eight years married to these three women and don't regret one minute.

Contents

PROLOGUE

PART I: AN EGG IS LAID

PART 2: THE EGG HATCHES

PART 3: THE FLEDGLING BUILDS A NEST

PART 4: PEREGRINATIONS

Contents

PART 5: THE QUEST

PART 6: GREAT GREY OWL

REFLECTIONS

EPILOGUE

APPENDIX 1: THE BIRDHOUSE RULES

APPENDIX 2: A BIRDERS' GLOSSARY

APPENDIX 3: THE BIRDS

 *Indicates a definition, a parenthetical remark or an author's comment outside the narrative.*

PROLOGUE

THE WINDING ROAD TO OREGON

RULE 1
If you have goals worth pursuing, persist no matter what,
and you will be rewarded in kind.
(Although I cannot predict what kind.)

Since 2009, I had attempted twice to travel from Denver, where I lived, to Newport, Oregon, to do a pelagic bird trip – an ocean voyage to seek species not commonly seen on land. Despite having a busy medical practice and a family, I was accustomed to going on a "wild goose chase" every few months to seek new birds and get away from my stressful routine as a neuro-oncologist. These marine trips, while essential for birders like me who wish to achieve a respectable Life List, are always a risk, subject to the vicissitudes of weather and the unpredictable behavior of the birds. Still, this unpredictability makes such trips exciting; you never know what you will see – or not see. For example, I once woke up after an all-night trip to sea from San Diego to find the boat parked beside an enormous

Sabine's Gull

Fork-tailed Storm Petrel

Blue Whale, my only one. (Whales, unfortunately, are not eligible for one's Life Bird list.)

The main goal of the trip to Oregon was to spot my first Fork-tailed Storm-petrel, a small, robin-sized, and striking seabird with—you guessed it—a forked tail and plumage with striking shades of grey. (Most other storm petrels are black.) Two previous attempts had been thwarted by bad weather and poor luck. On the second attempt, I arrived at the dock on time, about 6 a.m., and noticed a somber atmosphere among my fellow birders, many of whom, like me, had traveled many miles at considerable expense for this opportunity. I asked what was going on, without wanting to hear the answer. Someone responded with resignation: "I guess it's too rough to sail." There were only a few people there. I assumed the others had left, so I returned to my lodgings and went back to sleep. When I returned to the dock later to do some birding, I discovered that the weather had improved, and the boat went out after all. I felt like an idiot and missed my birds which the other birders found easily.

In September of 2018, undaunted, I booked the same trip again for a third attempt. I went straight from work to the Denver airport to fly to Portland, where I would arrive close to 10 p.m., rent a car, drive about two hours to the coast, and then get some rest before arriving at the dock for departure. With a few minutes to spare before boarding my flight, I sat down at an airport bar for a meal and a martini. After ordering, I went to the washroom where my cellphone fell out of my pocket. It was only after returning to the bar that I discovered it was missing. I searched everywhere, including the men's room, where

I crawled around on the floor with no luck. At least no one took a photo of me groveling on the bathroom floor to post on social media.

Despite having no phone—and therefore no GPS—to navigate the winding roads from Portland to the coast, or to find my rented lodgings for the night in Newport, I was determined to reach my destination. It never occurred to me to cancel and return to the comforts of home; I was committed. While I couldn't call the motel for directions, and I couldn't let my wife, Aura, know my whereabouts along the way, I managed to borrow a cellphone from the bartender so I could warn her about my predicament.

I wasn't worried; I had all night before I was due at the dock for debarkation.

I stopped at gas stations for advice and finally reached my destination in a pea-soup fog several hours later than planned. I used the phone in the inn's office to call my concerned wife to tell her I had arrived. Two hours later, vertical, wide-eyed, fed, and heavily caffeinated, I was standing at the dock in the morning gloom. Despite everything, I was soon on the sea and excited about the prospects of the day. Our leader told us there were two large fish-processing vessels along the planned route, great attractors of seabirds that would improve our prospects significantly and pungently.

Once we reached our destination, we were surrounded by a treasure of seabirds. In addition to numerous stunning Fork-tailed Storm-petrels, my principal goal for this adventure, we were dazzled by several enormous Laysan and Black-footed Albatrosses and numerous handsome Sabine's Gulls circling the boat. While the boat idled in calm water, we watched, speechless, as these pelagic creatures circled until we were dizzy, mesmerized, and serene.

That evening, to celebrate the triumph, I had a wonderful meal of oysters and fresh fish in Newport, where I also discovered a cocktail called "The Last Word" that combines gin with green chartreuse (made exclusively by monks), maraschino liqueur, and lime. The cocktail seemed appropriate, since after three attempts, and despite my lost cellphone, I had finally gotten the "last word" on my elusive Storm-petrel.

On my flight back to Denver, I wrote down the whole experience, the good and the bad, which I thought were of equal importance. The words seemed to flow effortlessly, and there was more to it than just finding my bird. That is when I decided to write about my alter life as a birder and address the issue of why I had such a passion for birding. I didn't realize that, within just a few months,

I would be retired from the medical profession during the COVID pandemic and living in Cape Breton, Nova Scotia, where I could concentrate on birding and writing.

This book is the result: a true account of 52 years as a birder, and the many lessons learned from my adventures.

The story begins in Colorado, where I met Dr. Michael Linshaw, an inveterate birder and photographer, who persuaded me to "do a little birding". I did and was hooked for life. After two years in Colorado chasing its trademark gallinaceous (chicken-like) birds, the story follows the chronology and itinerary of my medical career to Georgia, Los Angeles, Albany, N.Y., and back to Colorado, where I spent the next 32 years.

I recount my many birding forays to hotspots including Arizona, the Rio Grande Valley of Texas, Florida, Alaska, and ultimately the Canadian Maritimes. These episodes are grouped primarily by geography, but they are chronological within each region. I have fictionalized selectively to protect the innocent and the guilty.

Finally, I abruptly retired from medicine during COVID and fled to our home in Cape Breton, Nova Scotia, where I could devote myself to something other than medicine and family. This is where I resolved to pursue the goal of joining an elite and small group of birders who have seen 800 species of birds in North America. From this point, the book focuses on the adventures and the birds that are part of that quest.

The saga is divided into six parts based on my growth as a birder, each with several episodes, all preceded by a "rule." These rules are lessons learned and observations gleaned along the way, which collectively address the question, often asked by non-birders, of why a grounded physician with a family would pursue birding with such passion.

It is my hope that the adventures in these pages will help you understand this passion, that as we travel together from Atlantic to Pacific, from Mexico to the Arctic, you'll enjoy the triumphs and frustrations, the nature and scenery—and most of all, the birds—as though each were your own.

WHAT A BIRDER IS AND ISN'T

RULE 2
Never begin a book with a glossary or definition.
(You might sound pedantic.)

What is a birder? It's a good question with many answers. Let's start with the basics: Birders are people who are interested enough in birds to look for them.

Bird: A vertebrate that is not an amphibian, a reptile, a fish, or a mammal; all have feathers, and most have wings and can fly, while a few hapless species have grown flippers instead of wings and spend a good deal of their time on the ground where they are likely to be eaten, shot, or run over by a birder.

I think we can all agree on that. Birding can range from enjoying what appears on a backyard feeder to chasing the record for most species seen in the world, and everything in between.

For those of us on the more ambitious end of the spectrum, you might ask: *why are we so captivated by the avian kind?* This is a more challenging question.

First of all, there is not always an identifiable reason for such things. Why do some men wear shoes without socks? It might come down to DNA, over which we, of course, have no control. I won't bore you with the "nature versus nurture" conundrum: I've observed that an interest in birding is seldom, if ever, taught. I have four children, four grandchildren, two stepchildren, and two step-grandsons.

I am married for the third time, not uncommon among birders and physicians, and none of my children or spouses, despite my best efforts, has ever become a birder.

That does not mean they have never been with me on birding adventures or don't enjoy seeing something pretty, rare, or "cute." Several episodes in this book are about seeing birds with my family, and while they did not seek these experiences, they have never forgotten them. Why then did none of them join the club? Your guess is as good as mine, but there is some manner of switch in the brains of birders that non-birders lack and cannot acquire.

So, if being interested in something (though the word "interested" can be a monstrous understatement) is primarily not learned, then there must be something about each birder (genotype) that, under the right conditions, leads to the birding phenotype. There are probably countless "birders" out there who don't realize they are birders, because they were never inspired, or just not exposed. Others likely have the interest, but are embarrassed to "come out."

Under the right conditions, I might have known I was a birder from an early age. I grew up in Ohio, not far from some of the prime birds and birding spots in North America, such as Point Pelee on the north shore of Lake Erie and Kirtland's Warbler country in central Michigan. I was required to write a report on local birds in my early education. I went out and enjoyed finding as many local birds as possible, but didn't continue after the report was written. I suspect that if I had pursued any form of bird finding and admitted it, I would have been labeled a "sissy" or worse in the homophobic jock culture in which I grew up. Perhaps, therefore, I suppressed my natural inclinations. I was also hampered by a lack of interest in photography, which I unfortunately never learned or even really tried until recently.

The missed opportunities abound. I attended Cornell University in Ithaca, New York, and no birder needs to be told what a shame it is that I never took advantage of the iconic Cornell Ornithology Lab there—or even knew that it existed. It wasn't until 1972 at age 27 that I met Dr. Michael Linshaw, an avid birder and bird photographer, and became a card-carrying birder myself. He showed me some of his photographs and invited me to accompany him on a birding trip. I went, got hooked, and never looked back.

What caused this sudden and unexpected conversion? At the time, I had no idea. I just knew that I wanted to do it. In the years of birding that followed, I gradually acquired a better understanding of why I was so motivated, and the education is ongoing.

During my days of intense medical education, relative poverty, and the responsibility of being a husband and the father of two young children, my new interest provided an escape from the stresses of medical practice into the less predictable and regimented world of Nature, where I had no responsibility other than to be there. There are certainly other scenarios and motivations that lead people to commit to birding, but I'm confident that many birders share at least some of my story.

I probably don't need to tell you that my new zeal to seek and learn about birds came into conflict with the other imperatives of my life. I had plenty of things to do that interested me, and I didn't need another.

But there was no turning back. Once a birder, always a birder—regardless of the consequences.

I have never been what I consider a "good" or "legitimate" birder. I don't go out often, don't keep good field notes, and am certainly not an expert in identification. On the other hand, I have been an opportunist, having lived in several places where many species of birds could be seen. I have birded with and been taught by the best.

The late Arnold Small comes to mind, as well as Kimball Garrett, Hugh Kingery, Larry Manfredi, and Melody Kehl. (Separate chapters in this memoir are devoted to Melody and Larry.)

Once in Nova Scotia, my skills were improved by several local birders, including Steven McGrath and Dr. Ken McKenna. I am also blessed with the requisite capacity to be undeterred by hardship and disappointment.

Birders, often profiled as oddballs lacking in social skills, are not given proper credit for their ability to navigate the many barriers to successful birding. Many have paid a great price for their obsession.

More about that later, but I refer you to the book To See Every Species of Bird in the World, A Father, a Son, and a Lifelong Obsession by Dan Koeppel about his father, Morris Koeppel.

Often, the barriers are money and time, but even for those who have enough of both, serious birding can be a challenge to all one's faculties. I have had a long and successful career in medicine and have met many impressive colleagues, but I wouldn't put any of them ahead of the truly great birders that I know and admire.

We should clarify one thing: birders seldom "watch" birds, and the term *birdwatcher* is inaccurate and often pejorative. Although there are times when more prolonged observation is required for identification, or desirable because of a particular behavior, lingering too long "watching" one bird is likely to result in missing other birds, or being run over by oncoming vehicles driven by birders. It also might disturb the birds, who have a right to some privacy, especially during breeding season.

There are many levels of birderdom, from casual to fanatical, and there is a stereotype of the typical birder that includes drab and formless clothing, outlandish hats and vests, backpacks to carry field guides, binoculars, cameras, and all manner of unnecessary paraphernalia. Nearly all birders keep life lists of the birds they have seen. This can be carried to an extreme, and some listers give the rest a bad rap.

 *Lister: Nothing to do with mouthwash, someone who keeps a list or lists of birds seen. This can range from one's backyard, bathtub, state or province, country, or the world. This term can be used in a derogatory way to describe birders who are less interested in the birds than in the list(s).*

I'll admit a tendency toward eccentric behavior, such as the wearing of patches to let the world know where we have been, as if anyone cared. But not all of us birders are lunatics. Most birders are gentle, hospitable folks who are more than pleased to assist other birders and share their joy. *Eccentric* is probably the best word to characterize birders: people who are different enough to be more comfortable with Nature than people.

So what makes a birder?

In short, we are not easily classifiable people; we love the experience of finding elusive winged creatures for any number of reasons. There are certainly dark sides to birding: one-upmanship, over-competitiveness, ruthlessness in pursuit of goals, dishonesty, selfishness, neglect of people and responsibilities, bad hygiene, and bad manners. But these are universal qualities that we encounter in any arena that involves humans.

Perhaps that's it: birders wish to escape from the negatives of human behavior and "civilized life" in quest of something natural, fragile, elusive and free. It has been said before, but I'll repeat it anyway: It's usually not the outcome that matters most; it's the process. I calculate that I have traveled more than 100,000 miles for birding and have had innumerable unforgettable adventures along the way.

Of course, it never hurts when we find what we seek…
Enough said. Let's start birding.

PART 1

AN EGG IS LAID

BIRDING IN COLORADO, WHERE IT ALL STARTED

RULE 3
Pride is a paralytic poison
that kills relationships.

We arrived at the lek at dawn. To avoid spooking the birds, Michael and I took up positions at a considerable distance, but within range of our scopes and binoculars. Lek is the name given to the communal breeding sites of several species of chicken-like birds like the Greater Prairie Chickens that we hoped to see that day. These sites are usually located in remote and wild places that provide both a platform for breeding performance and adequate cover for security. It was the early spring of 1973 in Colorado— bitterly cold and windy, and we would have no shelter or respite for hours. Once the birds arrived, we were required to stay until they dispersed. Despite our discomfort, we were excited. Soon, we heard some clucking in the low bushes around the elevated lek. Then a couple of prairie chickens flew in and landed in the open. More birds arrived until there were about twenty. They began to strut, and the males displayed their distended orange neck bladders as they made sounds like air escaping from a balloon. The females pretended not to be interested, but they weren't fooling anybody. If they weren't interested, why would they be there at dawn on such a raw day? Finding this rare and elusive bird was one of the most memorable among the many adventures that I had in Colorado as a newly fledged and highly motivated birder.

Early in my pediatric training at The Children's Hospital in Denver from 1971 to 1974, I met Dr. Michael Linshaw. In addition to teaching me all I know about kidneys—which are important if you don't have them, but of lesser interest to me since I have two—Mike was my introduction to the world of birding.

I started going solo in the morning before work, usually before sunrise (regrettably when nearly all birding begins) to a small pond in the Bow Mar suburb of Denver, and the ponds at City Park. I identified numerous common wintering birds, mostly ducks and geese, but at the beginning of a birder's life, every new bird, no matter how common and mundane, is like a miracle. Ordinarily, it takes years to reach the point when new birds are seldom seen. Once that happens, however, the reduced frequency of new bird sightings is replaced by the exhilaration of finding more elusive birds, especially those birds that require the most effort to see.

I was off to a good start, complemented by numerous trips to visit Mike's friends, the Brockmans, in Evergreen, Colorado. They were a jovial and warm couple who had many feeders at which I saw a variety of forest birds, including all the races of Dark-eyed Junco that, at that time, were four separate species. The Brockmans adored Michael, who was not shy about requesting refreshments. He would ask, "How's that hot cider coming along?" as he walked through the door. The junco was my first, but only one of several birds that were once classified as separate species until being lumped into a single species by the American Ornithological Union (AOU) early in my days as a serious birder.

Conversely, there are many examples of birds that have been split into two or more species. While these separations are likely to make birders happy, they often require re-finding birds that had been split. This episodic lumping and/or splitting adds to both the pleasure and the inherent frustrations of birding. Incidentally, there is now talk, fifty

years or so after their lumping, to re-split the Yellow-rumped Warbler. The most recent loss was the Hoary Redpoll, now lumped with Common Redpoll into Redpoll. At the same time, the Herring Gull was split into American and European, a birders' wash.

I spent two years birding in Colorado before moving to Georgia in 1974. During that time, I began to compile a respectable list of life birds. At first, these were mostly yard birds, such as American Robins and House Finches, but I joined the Denver Field Ornithologists (DFO) which was a group of avid local birders, some of whom, like Harold Holt and Thompson Marsh, were widely known and, in the case of Harold, extraordinarily cantankerous.

Thompson was an excellent example of the unexplained tendency for birders to have names related to birds or nature, like Finch, Crow, or, famously, Phoebe Snetsinger, who saw 8398 species of birds in her lifetime. I am guilty of the same behavior; I named my only son Robin.

The DFO conducted excellent field trips that encountered many uncommon birds and provided valuable skills to novice birders like me. When a species was spotted, someone would announce its presence and support the accuracy of the identification by describing the key findings and field signs, as well as the location of the bird. For example: "There's a White-breasted Nuthatch on the trunk of that blue spruce. Notice its beeping call and its tendency to be upside-down as it feeds!"

Of course, large groups of birders often include those who manage to degrade the experience for others in a variety of ways. As my confidence grew, I tended to bird alone or with one or two companions with whom I had some rapport — often Mike or one of his friends, to avoid these distractions. This can be interpreted as snobbery, and sometimes it is, but it improves birding success.

Among the highlights of my early birding days in Colorado were the Rosy-finches. The three species of these finches have in common an unusual rose color, which gives them their name. They prefer cool mountainous locations near the tree line or, in the case of Alaska, non-mountainous places with cold temperatures. Although they can be found in several western states, Colorado is the best place to see all three species, which include the Brown-capped, Black, and Grey-crowned Rosy-finches.

Many birders come to Colorado in search of these elusive birds, and I was fortunate to be on a field trip that targeted them. It was winter, the time of year when the finches are most frequently found since they come to lower elevations to feed. In summer, the road we took goes all the way to the summit of Mount Evans, an elevation of more than 14,000 feet (over 4,300 m). In winter, it is kept plowed up to Echo Lake, at 11,000 feet (or more than 3,300 m). This road would later become one of my favorite routes for long climbs on my bicycle.

We were headed for Squaw Pass, (a name that I am certain will be changed soon), just below Echo Lake, where there is a weather tower and where we had heard that Rosy-finches were seen. We arrived and made it up the access road with some difficulty. Once we were on foot and armed with our binoculars, we spotted a large flock of birds showing the diagnostic rose color; they accommodated us by perching on the tower. We quickly discovered, much to our amazement, that all three species were present. Even the most jaded members of the group were surprised and elated. As a novice, I was unaware of how much traveling and searching might ordinarily be needed to see these three rare finches, requiring a trip to high mountains in winter or freezing Arctic tundra. Years later, I would encounter Black Rosy-finches above the tree line in Yosemite National Park on a solo hike when a sudden downpour forced me to take refuge under some overhanging rocks. As I sat waiting for the rain to subside, a flock of Black Rosy-Finches landed next to me, no doubt also seeking relief from the cold rain. Unlike me, they did not seem to have anxiety about the possibility of being stranded by weather above the tree line. They wandered around my feet as though I weren't there, completely unafraid. I'm sure they had never been that close to a human.

Years later, on a trip to Alaska in the spring, I saw innumerable Grey-crowned Rosy-finches nesting in the tundra and singing their hearts out, which I had never heard before, since most birds don't sing in winter. Since my first experience with Rosy-finches in the early 1970s, I have lived with the fear that they might be "lumped" into one species. So far, I have been spared.

The most sought-after family of birds in Colorado is undoubtedly the gallinaceous birds. These are game birds that resemble chickens—some are actually called chickens (Lesser and Greater Prairie Chickens). They share the characteristic of giving birth to chicks that, once hatched, immediately become mobile and are never helplessly confined to a nest. There are 13 species of these birds in Colorado: ten species of quail and grouse which occur naturally, and three— Wild Turkeys, Ring-necked Pheasants, and Chukar—which were introduced for hunting and have established nesting populations. There are annual organized birding trips to Colorado to see all these birds. It requires ten days and several thousand miles of driving to accomplish this goal. I was fortunate enough to live in Colorado long enough to see them one at a time, more comfortably and intimately. These adventures are among my most cherished during my 30-plus years as a Coloradan.

The first of the gallinaceous birds that I saw was the Greater Prairie Chicken. These strange, primal-looking creatures are found in remote areas of the short-grass plains of Colorado and a few adjoining states. They are scarce and threatened due to loss of habitat, and because they were once widely hunted for their meat. (This was illegal by the time I hit the prairies, and so the bird never landed on our table. As Tevye said in *Fiddler on the Roof*, "The only time a Jew eats a chicken is when one of them is sick.")

I was part of a field trip in search of the Greater Prairie Chicken, and Michael Linshaw, as always, was part of the group. As we crept along the off-road track in separate cars toward the lek, we were looking for other birds. Suddenly, the line of cars stopped, but I didn't notice until I had minimally dented Mike's back bumper. These low-speed fender benders are common among birders, but he was not pleased. Later, as we drove together in my car, I ran out of gas in the middle of nowhere. Once again, he seemed perturbed. Perhaps these events, which seemed trivial at the time, were harbingers of more serious problems in our future relationship.

Since that day in the early 1970s, the number of these birds has continued to decline. A few remain but can be seen only in the presence of a guide from the Department of Fish and Game, if you are lucky enough to get a permit. Many of the farmers on whose land the chickens still live have become advocates for the survival of those they haven't already eaten. The extinct Heath Hen, a subspecies of the Greater Prairie Chicken, which once strutted the leks of Massachusetts, was not as fortunate.

The next gallinaceous bird I saw was the White-tailed Ptarmigan. This bird lives above the tree line in the Rockies and turns snowy white in winter. It is easiest to locate in early spring when there are patches of residual snow. The birds gravitate to the snowy areas where they are less conspicuous. The strategy is to find such an area and trek from patch to patch looking for white lumps. There are two other species of ptarmigan in North America, Willow and Rock Ptarmigans, both seen in the Arctic tundra of Alaska and Canada.

For the White-tailed Ptarmigan, Mike and I, along with some other inveterate birders, took a winding and treacherous road to the top of Guanella Pass, about 50 miles west of Denver. Sure enough, we found an area of partial snow coverage near the parking lot and trailhead at the top. The group spread out to cover as many patches as possible while staying in sight of one another. It wasn't long before Mike and I noticed a few lumps in one of the patches. We got closer and then Mike shouted, "Ptarmigans! Ptarmigans!" While this was accurate, it was perhaps a bit too loud, no doubt an indication of an adrenaline rush. We noticed the thin red eyebrows and dark eyes of what otherwise looked like a white snowball of fluff.

Fortunately, ptarmigans are dangerously tame around humans and were not disturbed by Mike's enthusiasm. Our fellow birders confirmed a covey of them in striking winter plumage for everyone to see and photograph. Mike and I were thrilled to have spotted the birds in the company of some very accomplished birders. We were very lucky to find these birds so quickly. It might have taken hours, or we might have missed them altogether. The terrain was challenging as well, with willow tangles and icy patches of unstable snow. We were near the summit of Mount Bierstadt, one of Colorado's "Fourteeners," mountain peaks of 14,000 feet or more.

Fifty-eight mountains in Colorado exceed fourteen thousand feet. Many summits can be reached by walking up a trail, while others are technical and treacherous. Many mountaineers try to climb them all, and there is a record for doing so: 9 days, 21 hours, and 51 minutes.

Who, other than a birder, is crazy enough to be traipsing around such a treacherous place? Why do we take such risks and embrace so much discomfort? I think it is because birders are often loners and struggle to find camaraderie. These extremes foster connection, and we go to such lengths, in part, to be with other like-minded people.

The last member of the chicken-like family of birds that I saw before departing for Georgia was the Greater Sage Grouse, a large

White-tailed Ptarmigan

Brown-capped Rosy-finch

grouse that inhabits upland prairies dominated by wild sage. That is probably why it is called a sage grouse. However, there is no *Lesser* Sage Grouse, so I cannot explain the qualifier *Greater*. I saw this bird, again with Mike, in an area of Colorado called North Park.

It was spring, but we awoke in a high-altitude blizzard. We saw a couple of Greater Sage Grouse huddled under sage bushes, looking as miserable as we were before we made a run for Denver. We survived, but it took about nine hours instead of three or four. My parents were visiting at the time and were nearly catatonic with worry when I finally walked through the door. This confirmed their long-held suspicion that "our son the docta" was a lunatic. Nevertheless, I had indeed seen the Greater Sage Grouse. Sadly, I missed its mating dance; I'm certain I was not as sad as the birds.

My first wife, Irene, and I were blessed with our second daughter, Rebecca, on December 17, 1972. I was in the emergency room that night and scheduled to participate in my first Christmas Bird Count the next morning. This is an annual international event that was started in the days of Audubon in the nineteenth century, when it was the custom to shoot and record as many species of birds as possible. Despite the carnage, it was a valuable way of keeping an eye on worldwide bird populations. Now, we are more likely to shoot each other than the birds. I had never done it before and was very excited.

Just as I was about to be picked up before dawn to look for owls, I got a call from Irene: She was in labor. Another few minutes and I would have been in the woods with no means of communication, as there were no cellphones in those days. I would have missed the birth and probably would never have been forgiven. I went straight to the hospital as Irene was heading to the delivery suite. Rebecca was born a few minutes later.

Nearly missing Rebecca's birth is only one example of the many times birding came into conflict with my professional and personal lives. Many birders face this dilemma. I chose to put family and career first, which limited my development as a birder. Nevertheless, I kept at it and benefitted from the various places that we lived and the occasional opportunity to go on a junket to find rare birds.

The Greater Sage Grouse was the last of the game birds I saw in Colorado before my pediatric training was interrupted by two years of service in the Army Medical Corps during the last phase of the Vietnam War. I had signed up for the Berry Plan, a program that allowed physicians to defer obligatory military service until they had completed medical school and residency training. However, I could practice my specialty, pediatrics, instead of risking combat service. I was philosophically opposed to the war, but willing to care for the children of the soldiers. Irene, our two daughters, Jennifer and Rebecca, and I packed our belongings into our little yellow Datsun wagon and headed for Augusta, Georgia, home of the Masters Golf Tournament and Fort Gordon Army Medical Center, later the Eisenhower Army Medical Center.

It was painful to say goodbye to Mike. I saw him infrequently after I left Colorado. We were good friends and had enjoyed some great birding together. He was single at the time, and I had tried a few times to set him up since he was keen on finding a "chicken" (his term for "chick")with whom to start a family. He continued his training at the University of Pennsylvania and finally found the right "chicken," probably not on a lek, and was very quickly the father of two children.

Mike brought his family to visit me a few years later, 1977, in Los Angeles, and they stayed with us in our small rented house in Pacific Palisades. Unfortunately, he and his wife had two relentlessly demanding toddlers. These children, along with the new spouse, prevented Mike and me from enjoying each other's company as we had done in the past. As I had done, he had put his family first, but I felt deprived. He was single when we became friends, and things would never be the same. This, sadly, altered our friendship, although we had one sensational day of birding together when we left the kids and their mother behind. I didn't make any comments about the issue, but Mike could tell how I felt and was clearly and understandably offended.

We had minimal communication thereafter. In retrospect, if I had reached out, we might have saved our relationship. He was, after all, my birding inspiration and hero. He was a brilliant physician, scientist, musician, photographer, and birder. He never gave a medical lecture without showing a few bird photos and teaching something about the depicted birds. No one can fill the void that he left.

Pride, I've learned, is a paralytic poison that kills relationships. And for nongregarious people like me and most birders, lost friendships are extraordinarily painful. True friendships are rare and worth the effort to preserve, even if this requires putting the friendship ahead of less important issues.

YOU'RE IN THE ARMY NOW,
1974-1976

RULE 4
Give people *dan le-khat zekhut* (benefit of the doubt)
even if they talk funny, were enemies in the Civil War,
and use words like onest or twicet.

This very challenging virtue is encouraged, but not commanded in Judaism, but If you can do this, you will discover many surprising and mostly positive things about people.

In 1974, toward the end of the Vietnam War, I entered the Army Medical Corps as a pediatrician. I was assigned to Fort Gordon in Augusta, Georgia, instead of Walter Reed Military Hospital in Bethesda, Maryland, where I could have continued my fellowship training in pediatric hematology-oncology. I was not pleased with this interruption of my career, but I made the best of it.

I refused to do basic training. I was not about to risk my life carrying a rifle around at night in a swamp full of alligators and water moccasins to prepare myself to treat children with croup and impetigo. I arrived for my first day of patient care with a chip on my shoulder about being in the South. I was also missing various doodads required to be in proper uniform.

Sergeant Gerald Bedicek, my NCO, was alarmed. "Stay in your office, Doctor, and I'll fix you up. Don't leave for any reason." He returned shortly, pinned several mysterious doohickeys on my uniform (one looked like a snake wrapped around a telephone pole), and pronounced me "good to go."

Several mornings later, the corpulent and boisterous chief of pediatrics, Major Frank Roberts, returned from leave and rushed off, late as always, to the weekly meeting of department chiefs. A few minutes later, he returned, roaring his displeasure: "Bedicek! I know you had something to do with this!"

Bedicek had stolen the hardware off Major Roberts' uniform and transferred it to mine. I felt like a member of the cast of M.A.S.H., my favorite sitcom of all time. Each morning, when I arrived for duty at our clinic in a termite-infested World War II barracks, I was greeted by the resident Northern Bobwhite Quail. "Bob White," he would exclaim, and I would reply: "No, Major Arenson, if you please."

Sergeant Bedicek was certainly the most interesting character in our M.A.S.H. unit. He was responsible for acquiring anything that was needed to make things work with the limited resources provided by the Army. He showed up one day with enough paint to rehabilitate our grim surroundings and cheer everyone up a bit. This was an act of generosity toward the mothers and children whose spouses were predominantly deployed to Germany instead of Vietnam, perhaps because they were mostly military police. I suspected they were having the time of their lives while their wives were sweltering at Fort Gordon with the kids and nothing to do. Many did not have cars. Anything to cheer them up was laudable, including the paint. We all wondered how Bedicek had acquired the paint, which was a scarce commodity on base. We determined through the grapevine that he had made a trade involving surplus materials that we "didn't need." We all knew not to ask for more information, that what we "didn't need" was likely to be his next acquisition, and that what we "didn't know wouldn't hurt us."

Bedicek's entrepreneurial capers were complemented by some odd behaviors for which I can offer no explanation. He and his cronies would go into the woods at night with a pack of dogs, chasing raccoons. Once the unfortunate beast was treed and shot, the dogs would tear it apart. Bedicek would arrive for work in the morning, a bit ripe from his nocturnal adventures, but no one complained.

Bedicek was also famous for his imitations of soldiers showing up at daily sick call to avoid their unpleasant duty in the stifling heat and humidity. For example: "Doctor, I have a pain that starts raht about the ankle, then moves up m' layg, then jumps to the other layg, then gits round m' waist and feels jest lahk far, jest lahk far!"

The women were no better but had different complaints. I remember once being told, "Doc, I caynt go out in them woods today. I'm too dizzy."

"Are you spinning?" I asked.

"Yep, Doc, I sure am."

"Which direction," I asked, "clockwise or counterclockwise?"

"It's lahk the clock, Doc," one woman replied.

"OK, then," I said with conviction but little compassion, "Whenever the spinning starts, turn counterclockwise.

As for the "far," Bedicek's recommendation was that perhaps the fire department was a better place to have it treated. Humor, as you probably guessed, was the key to a bunch of Yankee doctors getting through two years in Georgia with our sanity intact, or at least no worse than when we started.

Just one more anecdote before I get to the birds. One of my pediatric colleagues was Dr. David Turberville. We got on well and pulled a few pranks on each other to keep our spirits up. I came in one morning for work and checked my schedule. There was a family of children coming in with lice. Our offices were also our examination rooms, so there was a considerable risk of bringing lice home to my own family. I asked the staff to put the kids in Dr. Turberville's office, since his schedule was open at that time. I was examining the infested children in his office when the good Dr. Turberville arrived, atypically early.

He asked, very appropriately, "Good morning, Dr. A. Why are you seeing these folks in my office?"

I replied in a businesslike manner. "Well, Dr. Turberville, these kids have lice, and I sure don't want them in mine."

Needless to say, he would eventually get revenge. He hid my hat one day, knowing that I spent my lunch hour at the gym where without it, I would be out of uniform. As I was leaving, my colleague Dr. Jim Kinney informed me that I would have to walk past the General without my hat, a heinous and punishable offense. I had to stay in the humid locker room for an hour before I could return to the clinic.

Raised in Ohio and educated in the Northeast, I was a Yankee in rural Georgia. I found myself in foreign territory from a cultural perspective and in a new habitat from a birding point of view, especially coming from Colorado.

 *When Richard Nixon resigned in disgrace from the Presidency, for example, my neighbors, most of whom were career military families, were grief-stricken, while I privately celebrated.*

I can't reminisce about Georgia without making a brief reference to my ex-wife Irene's exploits at the Augusta National Golf Club. She was a New Yorker with a bit of an attitude, which, in this case, I couldn't help but admire. She was well aware of Augusta National's discriminatory policies toward women, Jews, African Americans, and anybody else who wasn't a good old white boy. Fortunately, things have changed, at least a bit. In any case, she decided one day to express her indignation by driving her yellow Datsun wagon, which was stuffed with garden supplies and manure, into the Club. She was accompanied by my mother (also a New Yorker with an attitude), and they were immediately stopped by the club's armed guards, who told them that they must leave immediately. Irene drove toward the gate, made a U-turn, and headed back into the Club, where she was then threatened with arrest.

She finally left, after telling the guards, "I was just checking the place out in case I decided to join." We got a good laugh out of that, but I don't think the guards shared our amusement.

Back to the birds. I quickly discovered that my yard was inhabited by Carolina Wrens, one of the noisiest but most charming birds I have ever encountered. It is this bird that is heard loudly and incessantly singing in the background during the Masters Golf Championship. Brilliant red Northern Cardinals cluelessly pecked at their own reflections in my picture window. At night, we heard Chuck-will's-widows and occasional calling Barred Owls, all in harmony with a chorus of cicadas and tree frogs, and Pine Warblers aptly nested in our pines.

I joined the local Audubon Society and went on field trips, which usually focused on the Old Lock and Dam Park on the Savannah River. This was a birder's paradise inhabited by numerous southern specialties. The best bird, in my opinion, was the nesting Swainson's Warbler. These warblers are much sought after by birders not fortunate enough to live where they nest. While the warblers do nest in much of the southeastern United States, their numbers are sparse, and they are found primarily in canebrakes, where bamboo grows near fresh water. When nesting, they are most easily found by their song, since they are otherwise likely to be concealed in their damp habitats, which they share with unpleasant creatures like chiggers (biting mites) and water moccasins (a poisonous snake). The Swainson's Warbler's song is a distinctive *whee-whee-whee-whip-poor-will*, with emphasis on the last syllable.

I learned to find this bird predictably enough that I was given the honor by the local Audubon Society of showing it to birders attending the Georgia Birders' Convention. It was the first and last time I ever did this, and I was able to show this difficult bird to many who had never seen it before. I had never seen it either, until I moved to Georgia, and I didn't see it again until I saw several at Garden Key

Chuck-will's-widow

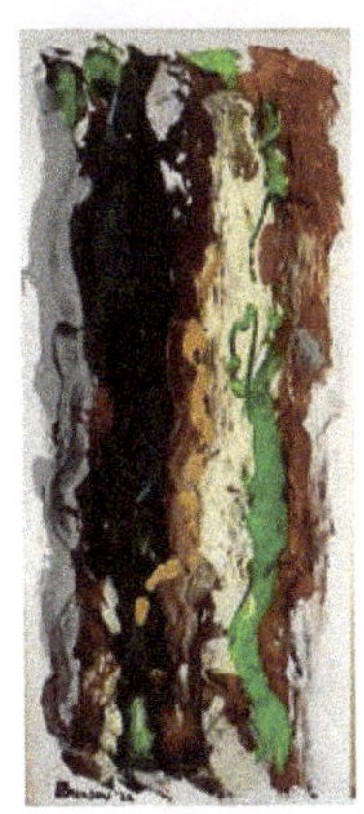

Palette Abstract of Swainson's Warbler
and Chuck-will's-widow

in the Dry Tortugas. It is always more satisfying, however, to see birds in their natural habitat, where they are more likely to be singing. To show the birds to others and to witness the birders' excitement and appreciation is especially gratifying and, for me, sets this particular warbler apart from many other uncommon birds that I have found.

As I birded with and became familiar with my new Georgian friends, I encountered a phenomenon with which I was previously unfamiliar — the constant and well-meaning effort to get me to join their churches and thereby become a legitimate member of the community. It seemed to me that my name and appearance should have been enough for them to deduce that I was Jewish, but that was not the case. I didn't want to shock them out of their ignorance, so I didn't press the point; I simply made excuses. In retrospect, that was probably the wrong strategy. They never really knew who I was, and I, as a result, never really got close enough to understand them. Perhaps the current political discord dividing rural and urban, north and south, has been fueled by such innocent but mistaken behavior.

I had arrived in Georgia with a chip on my shoulder about the South and Southerners. I came to understand they were just like anyone else—products of the culture in which they lived. Most were gracious and friendly, and their hospitality stood out in contrast to the large cities of the North, where "hospitality" means not being run over by a cab as you cross the street in your wheelchair.

As far as the genteel Southern spirit is concerned, I was fortunate to make the acquaintance of Gerald Knighton, a very skilled and active local birder. He was a true Southern gentleman, something

Swainson's Warbler   Prothonotary Warbler

that is noteworthy and praiseworthy about the Old South. He was gracious enough to take me to a park south of Augusta, where there was a growth of primal loblolly pines, the favorite habitat of the Red-cockaded Woodpecker. This was a life bird for me, and it is rare and local.

We walked for literally hours in search of this elusive woodpecker. Our strategy was to find an active site by looking for pine sap dripping from a nest, which the birds create yearly and which accounts for the dripping sap. We finally found a nesting site and waited and waited and waited some more. We were rewarded eventually with good looks at this coveted bird, which needed at that point to return to its nest as much as we needed to return to ours.

On my own, I undoubtedly would have checked for the bird and quickly gone elsewhere if I hadn't found it immediately. And I would have missed the bird if I had taken that approach. Thus, Gerald had taught me that patience pays off in birding and, no doubt, in many other endeavors. Birders, including me, seem to be in a hurry and often play tapes of the bird's song or make stimulatory noises to attract the birds out of their cover. There is an infamous tape called the "mob call," which plays the hoots of a Screech Owl, accompanied by the alarmed response of other birds, especially chickadees. This excites any birds within hearing range and causes them to dart out of cover into plain sight. A better strategy is to wait for a bird to become acclimated to your presence until it reveals itself. This approach leads to a better look at an undisturbed bird as it goes about its business. If the bird has the time, we should too. This sighting of the Red-cockaded Woodpecker brought me to approximately 200 life birds.

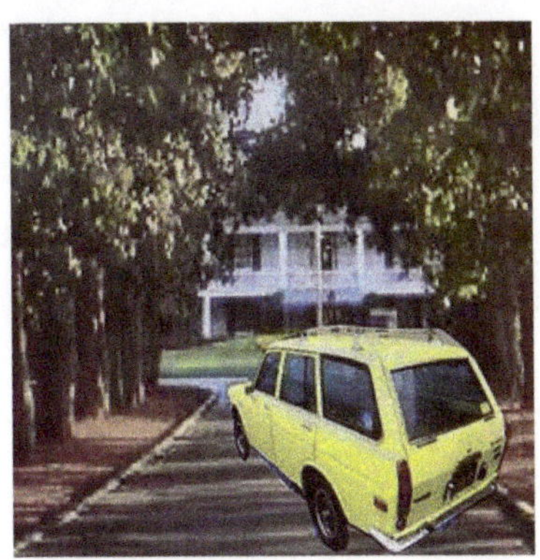

Irene's Yellow Datsun at the Augusta
National Golf Club

Least Bittern

Red-cockaded Woodpecker

My experience in the military was different from what I had expected. I had served my patients and, in doing so, my country. It is now my opinion that everyone should have an obligation to devote one or two years of service to their country, choosing from a variety of options. I believe this would create a much-needed sense of belonging and the likelihood of viewing government as a necessary evil rather than the enemy. Additionally, many people, especially young men, are not ready to take college seriously at age 18. An additional two years of service and maturity, before I matriculated at Cornell, might have led to a more valuable experience.

And with that consideration, I left the deep South, which I learned to admire for its gentility, literature, beauty, and hospitality. I was headed to Los Angeles, where I would complete my training at UCLA and experience yet another culture shock and a Noah's Ark of new birds. On the way, we took a slight detour.

RULE 5
When opportunities present themselves, seize them.

 *Second chances are rare. As the late philosopher and former Yankee catcher Yogi Berra reputedly said, "If you come to a fork in the road, take it.*

It was early summer, 1976. Irene and I were traveling with our two young children and everything we owned from Augusta, Georgia, to Los Angeles, where I would continue my training at UCLA. I managed to persuade Irene to take a "small diversion" to central Michigan, near Jackson, where we might get a chance to see the Kirtland's Warbler. At that time, the Kirtland's was critically endangered and down to about 200 pairs. They nested in an area where young jack pines were growing after a wildfire, the only habitat where this nitpicky warbler nests. Irene was a good sport about this escapade, which required us to travel about a thousand extra miles, but she has never let me hear the end of it. We have been divorced since 1984 and talk infrequently, but when we do, the subject always comes up.

We got up early and set off on our tour. The rangers were radiant with the joy of their task, and it was contagious. After only a few minutes of travel on a golf cart (with the compulsory ranger) into the sandy stand of Jack Pines, we heard the distinctive song of our bird, which ends with two emphatic notes preceded by a short but more complex prelude. Once the song was heard, it was simply a matter of a little patience to allow the bird to show itself, as there was not much foliage in which to hide. Our bird was very accommodating; its dark, masked face and yellow body quickly came into view.

My only regret was not being able to encounter this bird—the only Kirtland's Warbler I've ever seen—on my own and get acquainted less formally. This is one of the rarest birds I have seen and one of only a few of my *lifers* that have been saved from extinction. Unfortunately, I do not have a photograph as a memento, so I painted the bird instead. Irene, to whom I gave the original painting, which now hangs on her wall, claims that I hogged our single pair of binoculars so that she

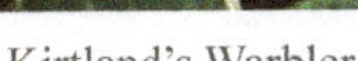

Kirtland's Warbler

Our Alternative Route
from Georgia to California

never got a good look at the warbler. For me, it was Life Bird 210, give or take a few, and a key moment in my birding career.

It had been worked out that the rapid and alarming decline of Kirtland's Warbler was related to two main factors. First, its nests were being parasitized by Brown-headed Cowbirds, which would lay their eggs in the warbler's tiny nest. Once the cowbird chick or chicks hatched, they were so much larger than the warbler chicks, and consumed so much food, that the warbler chicks would starve to death if they weren't pushed out of the nest first by the cowbird chicks. Second, forest management prevented the jack pines from burning. Without fire, jack pine seeds do not germinate, and no young trees grow. The warblers, much to their detriment, are very finicky and will not nest in the mature trees. That is why the Kirtland's Warbler is often referred to as the "firebird." Once these things were figured out by some very smart and determined biologists, a program was launched to reduce, quite brutally, the population of Brown-headed Cowbirds and to allow jack pines to burn, but under "control."

This plan went tragically wrong in 1980, when an attempted controlled burn, now known as the Mack Lake Fire, went wild. It consumed 44 homes and killed one young firefighter named James Swiderski. This tragedy led to a major upheaval of conflict and emotion in which the bird itself, rather than human error, was blamed for the catastrophe. This story was recently aired on National Public Radio, which conducted interviews with people on all sides of the discussion. Perhaps most importantly, the family of the lost firefighter harbored no resentment against the conservation efforts. On the contrary, they felt their departed kinsman was a hero who had participated in the successful preservation of one of the earth's most fragile but exquisite creatures. Now there are more than 2,000 breeding pairs, and the species is relatively safe—if any living thing is safe under present conditions.

There are still those who simplify the situation quite unfortunately, down to swapping a human life for a bird. This misses the point, but the human world is so anthropocentric that many are not interested in environmental issues. When such people wield power, it puts us all at risk, human and beast. The Kirtland's Warbler spends the winter in a few small Caribbean Islands, including Turks and Caicos, where they are also at the mercy of inhabitants and visitors with things other than bird conservation on their minds.

As for Irene and the kids, they still remember this "slight diversion" of about a thousand miles. They have come to value the timeliness and timelessness of this trip. It was one of those opportunistic adventures that my oldest daughter, Jennifer, has often said were among the fondest memories of her childhood, in retrospect, of course. Much of her early childhood would take place in Los Angeles where our lives as a family would change forever.

PART 2

THE EGG HATCHES

> **RULE 6**
> Anyone can make a difference,
> and any difference matters.

In the late 1970s, the status of the California Condor was critical. We were living in southern California at the time, Pacific Palisades to be precise, where from 1976 to 1981, I finished my training in pediatric hematology-oncology and started my academic career as an Assistant Professor at UCLA. There were only about 35 condors left, and they were not successfully breeding. I attended several contentious meetings of the Santa Monica Bay Audubon Society, during which the prospect of a captive-breeding program to save the species was hotly debated in the presence of those empowered to make the final decision.

There were valid opinions on both sides. On one side were those who believed we should not tamper with nature and that captive birds would die off in captivity. Even if they could breed in captivity—a complete unknown—what reason was there to believe the captive-bred birds would ever survive in the wild? On the other hand, other threatened birds, such as the Peregrine Falcon and Whooping Crane, had been saved by captive breeding programs.

Ultimately, the captive-breeding program for the California Condor was initiated in 1979 and has been modestly successful. At that time, however, we had no idea whether this majestic species would survive. Accordingly, the Santa Monica Bay Audubon Society, a group of capable if unconventional California birders of which I was an active member, organized an event we called the Santa Monica Bay Audubon Society Condor Watch and Tequila Bust. It was spring 1979. We would camp overnight on Mount Piños, north of Los Angeles, raise some hell, then drive to the observation area at the top of the mountain before sunrise to optimize the chance for a condor flyover.

Living in Los Angeles, we were financially challenged. As a junior faculty member, my new and bigger salary was only about $40,000 per year, not nearly enough to buy a suitable house. But I had the opportunity to work with the UCLA Bone Marrow Transplant Program, where we published an important paper demonstrating, for the first time, that successful bone-marrow transplants for leukemia were attributable to an immune attack against leukemia from the donor bone marrow—perhaps the first proof that the immune system could cure cancer.

That night, we experienced some moderate revelry, enhanced by the appearance of a family of indignant but curious Spotted Owls, also endangered, which responded well to my best hooting efforts and spent the evening hooting back at me and other revelers from perches around the campsite.

Early in the morning, before first light, and nursing headaches from the previous evening's campground transgressions, a group of about 20 inveterate birders and family members, including my wife, Irene, and daughters, Jennifer and Rebecca, ascended Mount Piños in our cars. We parked in the observation area at the top and stepped out into the chilly dark, where we shivered, paced, and waited for sunrise. At least that part was predictable. The sun did rise, as anticipated, in a cloudless and empty sky. We continued to pace and scan the nearby ponderosas, but there were no roosting condors in sight. Eventually— surreally—specks appeared high over the plains to the east. They grew larger as they approached our lookout.

We held our breath in hopes that these dots would get close enough to identify. We never imagined they would fly directly overhead, as they did, perhaps 50 yards above. With craned necks, we stared in silence and disbelief at five gigantic red-headed black and white birds with primaries flared in classic condor fashion. When it finally sank in that we had seen five of the last thirty-five wild California Condors on earth, we lost our composure and dour birding demeanor and began shouting, whooping, and jumping up and down like a pack of chimpanzees behind a banana truck. It was pure, unbridled joy. Moments like this are rare—usually associated with the birth of a child, winning the Stanley Cup, or completing *Moby Dick*. Those lucky enough to have experienced something like this will better understand why birders do what they do.

Jennifer and Rebecca have never forgotten this experience, although neither ever took up serious birding. Recently, we made a video for the PBS series "Story Corps" to archive this event, which remains indelible or, or mostly indelible, as there are some disputed points between my ex-wife and me. California Condors now inhabit the wild again, and seeing one would be a thrill, but not quite the same as the thrill we felt that morning. After declining further to just nine wild birds in 1986, the California Condor's status has been changed from endangered to threatened. There are more than 400 of these birds in the wild now, at several locations.

Mount Piños is also a favored site for finding White-headed Woodpeckers and Mountain Quail, which, like love, are not rare but seldom found when you're looking for them. This is where I enjoyed my last birding experience with Dr. Michael Linshaw, and those are the birds we found. In addition, we noticed the persistent squawking of a group of Steller's Jays. As this often indicates the presence of an owl, we decided to investigate. Sure enough, we found a Spotted Owl perched in a tree, with a cadre of Steller's Jays harassing it.

During my years living in Los Angeles, I had other rich birding experiences. California is one of the birding hotspots in North America, and I took full advantage. I signed up for a field ornithology course at UCLA, taught by the late and incomparable Arnold Small. We found and identified most of the nesting and migratory California birds and discovered many wonderful birding spots, including a special and little known oasis in the Mojave Desert called Butterbredt Springs, where in the presence of elusive desert birds such as Lawrence's Goldfinch, Grey Flycatcher, and Black-chinned Sparrow, I began a relationship with Julie, the woman who would become my second wife.

My first pelagic birding expedition was part of Arnold Small's course. This involved many hours at sea looking for species of

Spotted Owl

California Condor

birds that are seldom, if ever, seen on land. The trip was transcendent. We sailed to Santa Barbara Island, the westernmost of the Channel Islands, which stretch from San Diego to Santa Barbara. One of these is Santa Cruz Island, which is the only place in the world to see the Island Scrub Jay.

I saw this bird many years later after it was split from the California Scrub Jay.

Near Santa Barbara Island, we saw a Red-billed Tropicbird, one of the most iconic of all birds because of its rarity and unique appearance. We were dazzled by its snow-white body, blood-red bill, black facial mask, and long ribbon-like tail. While the more experienced birders on the boat politely expressed their good fortune to encounter this species, Arnold's students, most of us newcomers to birding at sea, looked like we were on an LSD trip. Once I had seen this spectacular bird at sea, I was hooked.

It was on subsequent pelagic trips on both coasts that I found myself in close quarters with some of the great birders of the day, including Debra Shearwater, Guy McCaskie, Kimball Garrett, and Bruce Pattison. Pelagic birding is not for the faint-hearted. The sea is unpredictable, conditions are often unpleasant, and trips are sometimes canceled. The surprises, which more than compensate for any discomfort, are not restricted to birds but include mammals, such as whales, dolphins, seals, and sea lions, fish, such as Basking and Whale sharks, and Ocean Sunfish, and various species of turtles, including huge Leatherback Sea Turtles that swim from New Zealand to California waters.

You may recall one overnight trip from San Diego I've already mentioned, when we awoke with an enormous Blue Whale beside the boat. Our boat was anchored so the crew could catch some fish for breakfast (perhaps my best breakfast ever); the whale must have been curious, as it stayed with us while we ate. This intimate encounter with the world's largest animal, a hundred miles west of the mainland over a reef that is a destination for "dudes" (surfing aficionados) was unforgettable.

There is an underwater mountain about 100 miles west of San Diego that attracts the prototypical California surfers like Sean Penn's "Spicoli" in the cinema classic, Fast Times at Ridgemont High. These teenaged dudes have long, stringy hair, sun-damaged skin, and a penchant for ditching high school classes when the surf's up.

Frequently, I traveled on Fridays after work from Los Angeles to Monterey to go pelagic birding with "Captain" Debbie Shearwater, one of the most talented, if not always warm and fuzzy birders I have ever met. I was often accompanied on these excursions by Terrence Whitley, a bright and eccentric Cal Tech student who, when he wasn't birding with his ancient monocular, spent his weekends in solitude in Death Valley at the helm of an electron telescope, trolling for extraterrestrial life.

We would depart for Monterey after work, stop for crab in Santa Barbara, sleep in the car in the parking lot at Fisherman's Wharf, arise at dawn for a delicious breakfast of eggs and calamari or homemade Italian sausage, board the boat for our trip, then drive back to Los Angeles the same day. We managed to see many California seabirds and other wildlife, all the while enjoying interminable conversations about the cosmos (and of course, women). We became experts and notable consumers of California produce, especially the wide variety of melons we found at roadside stands along the way. I bored him with the details of my medical research, most of which

Red-billed Tropicbird

amounted to naught, while he mused about finding alien civilizations in space.

The "techie" and I lost track of each other over the years, another example of a friendship lost from neglect. Those were tumultuous days in both our lives, softened considerably by our shared joy of pelagic birding, which I continue to this day, though not often enough.

To be honest, my memories of life in California are ambivalent overall. I matured as a physician. I saw many new birds and grew as a birder. But I'd be lying if I said my frequent travel and grueling hours at the hospital didn't contribute to the end of my first marriage.

Still, by the time I left California in 1982 to take a position at Albany Medical College, I had published a few important papers, one of which showed, for the first time, that bone marrow transplantation was the first proven use of immunotherapy to cure cancer. I had also added nearly two hundred more birds to my Life List, including the Yellow-billed Magpie, the only bird that is restricted to California, by its own choice.

If I had already set a goal of listing 800 North American birds at that time, I would have been about halfway there, after birding for just ten years. That comes to about 40 lifers a year.

The second 400 would be much more difficult.

NEW YORK AND NEW ENGLAND: THEY'RE FOR THE BIRDS

RULE 7
Don't let a day pass without experiencing beauty.

I f asked where the best birding areas are in North America, most birders would name Florida, Texas, Arizona, California, and Alaska. I have already added Colorado to that list, but here I'd like to make a minority case for the northeast coast, which has produced some of the most noteworthy rarities.

Before a Steller's Sea Eagle appeared in New Brunswick in 2021, the most famous was probably a Ross's Gull, which was found at Plum Island, Massachusetts in 1975. An Ivory Gull was in Plymouth Harbor, also in Massachusetts, a few years ago when, ironically, I was in Texas looking for other birds. A Red-footed Falcon was recently found, and a Little Egret has been seen yearly in Maine. Finally, a Great Black Hawk spent some time in Maine not long ago. I am sure there are many more. These rare birds, especially in populous regions, invariably draw hordes of twitchers, who will come from just about anywhere to find a rare bird.

Twitch: This describes the behavior, more or less unique to birders, of dropping everything at a moment's notice to dash off to see birds. An extreme example is a neurosurgeon at my hospital who left his post to chase a bird without arranging for anyone to cover his patients. He lost his license as a result. Other forms of twitching are not relevant to this book but are certainly important to those who are doing the twitching.

Twitcher: A birder who takes twitching to an extreme, which earns him or her this dubious description and often results in calamitous effects on earnings, relationships, and country club memberships, but does result in an impressive list of birds.

Since I lived in Colorado from 1987 until I moved to Cape Breton in 2020, I have spent limited time in New England, but I did live in Albany, New York from 1982 to 1988. Moreover, my two oldest daughters, Jennifer and Rebecca, both now married with children, live in Plymouth, Massachusetts, and Burlington, Vermont, respectively. Let's start with Albany.

I was at Albany Medical College as Section Head of Pediatric Hematology-Oncology after leaving UCLA in 1982. As I made the transition, it was becoming clear that the years of hard work by my colleagues and me had paid off, and we would soon be able to cure most patients with childhood leukemia and other pediatric cancers. This was one of the most monumental achievements in the history of medicine. I was in the right place at the right time, and I was grateful to be part of it. Now I could bring this experience to Albany, which lacked a fully trained pediatric oncologist to develop a state-of-the-art program.

My first wife Irene and I separated, and she moved to Ithaca, New York, about a three-hour drive on back roads from Albany, when there were no cellphones but only phone booths. I was on call continually for three years before recruiting a partner, so I had few opportunities to get away other than to see my children.

I was very busy, but I was vigilant, as always, for birding opportunities. I managed to get plugged into the birding community and added slowly but steadily to my list.

One day in the winter of 1984, I got word that a Northern Hawk Owl was roosting reliably on a wire in the Adirondacks. Additionally, a Hoary Redpoll was coming to a private feeder near Lake Champlain, and the owner was accepting birders by appointment. (Hoary relates to its pallor, not its sexual behavior.) These were both life birds for me, so I decided to make the drive on a Saturday in the old Honda CVCC I had bought in Los Angeles from prolific actor and former Cornell professor, Harold Gould. It was not an ideal car for winter driving in upstate New York and Vermont. I took the New York State Thruway north and turned west toward Lake Placid.

I already knew the town of Keene, home of the Noon Mark Diner, my watering hole after backpacks into the Adirondack High Peaks. As I pulled onto the town's main street, there— perched on a telephone pole, exactly where it was supposed to be!—was my Northern Hawk Owl. I wish other species were as accommodating. This is a truly rare bird, seen only irregularly in the boreal forests of Minnesota and Canada, and a few spots high in the Colorado Rockies.

I identified its tail, uniquely long for an owl, and its white face and yellow eyes.

Tail: Extends south from the rump when the bird is flying north.

I was thrilled, and I still had plenty of time to get to Vermont to look for the Hoary Redpoll. There was just one problem: The sky had been clear, but clouds were gathering, and the temperature outside was dropping, as was mine. The Honda's heater and I were both accustomed to being in California.

If you've never driven from New York State to Vermont in a blizzard, let me set the scene. There is a dramatic increase in snowfall with rapidly deteriorating visibility, a white-out. The windshield ices up because the defroster doesn't defrost. The car is cold because the heater doesn't heat. There is only a map, no GPS. And you are doing this to see a bird. If you don't survive, you are more likely to be the subject of ridicule than grief.

Somehow, I shivered through to the cabin in Vermont, where I was invited inside to warm up and watch the feeders. A little tea and the startling appearance of the Hoary Redpoll, a ghost-like white finch with a crimson crown, thawed me out. It would be 30 years before I saw my next one in Alaska.

Unfortunately, the Hoary Redpoll was recently lumped with the Common Redpoll into just Redpoll. I will keep the Hoary on my list, but begrudgingly not add it to my number of species. Ironically, the Herring Gull was also split into American and European species to make it a wash.

I was soon on my way back to Albany at an average speed of about 30 miles per hour in the growing blizzard. Miraculously, I arrived safely and was able to tell this story. I resolved then to get a new car that could be trusted in the northern winters, but on a pediatrician's salary minus alimony and child support, that would take years.

In spring, I learned about isolated locations in the rural areas near Albany where Henslow's Sparrows nested, one near the town of

Northern Hawk Owl

Hoary Redpoll

Westerlo, a northern "hollow" of Appalachia famous for its corncob backscratchers. Spring was the perfect time to look for this rare sparrow since it would be singing. When silent, this bird is seldom found. I traveled to the area described—a grassy field with some low bushes where the bird prefers to perch and sing. The song, or more accurately, the chirp, can be described phonetically as *tsi-lick* or *f-lee-sic*. It is soft enough to be obscured by other sounds, such as wind, insects, breathing, even whimpering to oneself, but I managed to hear it. Once heard, the bird can be found, with luck and patience, perching in the low shrubbery.

After some frustration, I finally spotted my bird and its flat, olive head. In contrast to its brown, scalloped back and white belly with a few brown streaks, its bill was pinkish and appeared large compared to the head, and it had a dark mustache.

Head: This speaks for itself.

Mustache: Some birds are described as having mustaches. This is fine for the males, but can be confusing to the females.

This is the only Henslow's that I have seen, although it is relatively common where I grew up in the Midwest before I became a birder. It is a prized bird on Christmas bird counts in Texas where it winters.

With this sighting, my Life List had reached approximately 500 birds. But once a birder gets to 500, new life birds start to become rare and costly. *Cost per bird*—or CPB—is a bit of regular birder jargon describing this situation.

Late in 1987, I moved from Albany back to Denver to lead the brain tumor team at The Children's Hospital. I would remain in Denver for 32 years until COVID forced me to retire. After moving to Colorado, my only trips to the Northeast were to see my daughters and grandchildren, but these visits still managed to produce many birding highlights.

The first of these was the shocking report on the North American Rare Bird Alert of a Boreal Owl roosting in a yew tree near the entrance to the Berklee College of Music in Boston. I was visiting my daughter, Jennifer, who was in graduate school at Harvard at the time. We easily found the owl, my only Boreal Owl so far, but even the absurdity of finding a rare Boreal bird in Boston didn't seem to boost Jen's enthusiasm. Conversely, I would have been thrilled to see the bird even if it were taking a course in evolutionary biology at Harvard. I have subsequently learned that the Boreal Owl is endemic but rare in the Canadian Maritimes, where I now live. As the crow (or owl) flies, this is not far from Boston, and I suspect our Berklee bird came from somewhere in Canada and made a wrong turn after eating too many fermented berries.

 *Ironically, the best place to find a Boreal Owl in the lower 48 states is in the mountains of northern Colorado, where I have yet to see one.*

A few years later, Jennifer was married and living near Plymouth, Massachusetts. It became an annual event to visit her and see my grandchildren, Annie and Ben, during spring break. We often rented a house on Martha's Vineyard near the town of Menemsha, which had a wonderful seafood market and eatery situated in a small harbor full of fishing boats. This shop made a smoked bluefish spread that is among the best things I have ever eaten. It was a good birding spot as well, and I always brought my binoculars to scan the harbor as I waited for lobsters to be cooked.

I routinely checked the nearby beach and jetty, where I often found common and occasional Red-throated Loons and some sea ducks, mostly Common Eiders, but on one such occasion, I saw some movement on the end of the jetty. I needed my scope, which

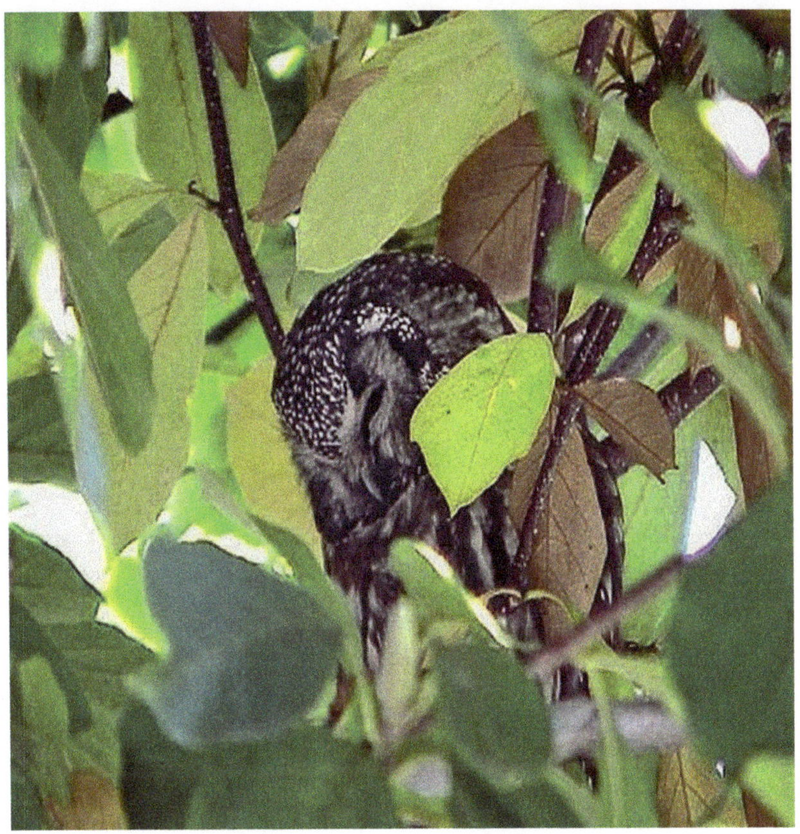

Boreal Owl in Boston - Photograph Provided by Marj. Rines

was fortunately in the car. I set it up and waited. The bird, which I suspected by habitat to be a Purple Sandpiper, was not cooperative. It only popped into sight for a second or two, not long enough to identify it yet, but enough to hold my attention. I had spent many hours in the past shivering on rocky shores looking for this winter shorebird without success, and I was determined not to miss it now.

While I waited, my grandchildren and adult family members patiently made the most of the beach to throw stones and dig. Ben, aged about two years old at the time, predictably ran down the beach butt-naked and pretended not to hear my daughter's frantic calls for his return. It was during this chaos that the bird—perhaps to assess the commotion—finally climbed to the top of the rock and revealed itself, as I had suspected, to be my first Purple Sandpiper with all the requisite markings: a droopy orange bill, orange legs, and a white eye ring.

Legs: With which a bird walks and to which are attached the feet, which, in the case of raptors, have talons to catch prey. Some birds are named after their legs, which people are not, e.g., Yellow-legged Gull or Rough-legged Hawk. Can you imagine someone being called a Red-legged Michigander?

Subsequently, on a fall visit to see my daughter Rebecca, whose new home and beach house were on Lake Champlain, we crossed the lake on a ferry and drove to Lake Placid for a short stay. I had many memories of this town in the Adirondacks. I had spent two summers there, newly married (for the first time), making fudge and getting ready for medical school. I wasn't yet a birder but loved the area's lakes, mountains, and streams, where I first learned to fly fish. In those early days I had never even heard of Bicknell's Thrush, the rarest of nesting thrushes in North America, whose habitat is restricted to stunted growth at the top of selected mountains extending from western Massachusetts to the Cabot Trail in the Cape Breton Highlands of Nova Scotia, and northern New Brunswick. Now, after many years of birding, I was aware the Bicknell's could be sighted near certain peaks in the region we were visiting.

One such spot is Whiteface Mountain, near Lake Placid, the top of which is accessible by car. I had driven up several times before, and we decided to do it now as an adventure for the grandchildren. The colors were New England spectacular, but the top was raw and windy. Rebecca, who is an endurance athlete and exercises for therapeutic respite, decided to run down the mountain and set out to do so despite the entreaties of her spouse. I impulsively decided to follow her, as I was also a runner, at least when there was a good reason to run. In this case, it was to share the exhilaration with Rebecca and escape the car for a few moments.

As we ran, I spotted some movement in the sparse mountaintop growth. These were undoubtedly thrushes, and I immediately thought of Bicknell's Thrush, because nothing much else lives there. We got a pretty good look at close range, but without binoculars. It was distinctly browner than Swainson's Thrush, which shares the same terrain. I thought it very likely we had seen a Bicknell's when I was not looking for it. The ranger at the station at the base of the mountain confirmed my suspicion, so I added it to my Life List as a provisional

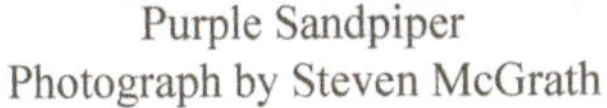

Purple Sandpiper
Photograph by Steven McGrath

Purple Sandpipers in Flight
Photograph by Steven McGrath

sighting, which would require a better one someday, preferably with song.

The years passed, and eventually my oldest two grandchildren were getting close to leaving the nest. It was 2017 and my third wife Aura and I were thinking about my retirement and where we could live to be closer to our children and grandchildren. We decided to consider Maine and arranged to meet Jennifer and her family near Bar Harbor in spring. After a nice visit, we were headed next to Vermont to visit Rebecca and her family too. The night before departure, I noticed a report of a rarity in Maine near the village of Damariscotta. We could try for the bird on our way.

After a couple of hours meandering through the back roads of Maine, we realized we were approaching our destination. I took my time to avoid getting lost, and we arrived in the picturesque village of Damariscotta as rain began to fall with increasing force. As our GPS announced we had arrived at our destination, we saw the steeple of the church described on the alert. My heart was racing: a Fieldfare was unanticipated and quite rare in North America. But I didn't know until later just how rare.

When we got to the church and parked, the rain was drenching and cold. We spotted the unmistakable group of birders huddled on a rise near a pond. Aura wisely decided to stay in the car while I grabbed my gear and raced to the pod of birders who told me our bird was present, after having been lost earlier in the day, and I should keep my eyes on the open ground near the trees by the pond. Within a few minutes, someone said, "There it is." And there it was. We all spotted it on the ground showing off its grey head, yellow eyes, brown back, and handsome spots on its flanks. I had my bird and was able to share my joy with my patient spouse, who, despite not being in "the club," somehow dryly understood.

Bicknell's Thrush

Piping Plover - Found and Photographed
at Duxbury Beach

Recently, I stayed with Jennifer at her home in Plymouth, Massachusetts for two weeks while I had surgery on my knee. Jennifer had discovered the Merlin app, which identifies birds by their calls and songs. Each morning at sunrise, I put my iPhone on the windowsill to record birds. I was shocked to discover a very impressive number of uncommon migrants and other secretive nesting birds. Jennifer contacted a local biologist at my request to determine if we might find calling Eastern Whip-poor-wills in the area. I needed the bird for my life list, since it had been split from the Mexican Whip-poor-will, which I had seen in New Mexico.

He suggested checking the Miles Standish State Forest, which we proceeded to visit at dusk with my granddaughter's likely future father-in-law, Keith Gizzi, who is not a birder but seemed very motivated to hear a Whip-poor-will for the first time. We were thrilled to hear several of these nocturnal birds where the Mayflower pilgrims and the Wampanoag people had once heard them. Keith was so excited that he doubled back after we parted to spend some private time with his new bird and thus acquired the nickname "Doubleback Gizzi." I'm certain that Longfellow's Priscilla Mullins would have said, "Sing for yourself, Keith."

A few days later, Jennifer and I took a stroll at Duxbury Beach, where we were thrilled to spend some quality time with a flock of endangered Piping Plovers and were attacked by nesting Least Terns, also endangered.

These annual family reunions, despite occurring at suboptimal times for birds, have produced at least three life birds, two of which I

Some of the Lucky Ones

Damarascotta Fieldfare:
Discovered, Photographed,
and Published by Jeff
Cherry, April 19, 2017
in The Boothbay Register

am unlikely to see again. Combining this with the joy of sharing these experiences with children and grandchildren greatly enhances their importance, and for that I am grateful.

It's another piece in the puzzle of the allure of birding.

PART 3

THE FLEDGLING
BUILDS A NEST

**COLORADO CALLS ME HOME,
1988-2020**

RULE 8
Not everything has an explanation, so accept the good
and bad as part of life, which itself has no explanation.

Late in 1997, after nearly six years in Albany, I was offered a faculty position at The Children's Hospital in Denver, where I had done the first three years of my post-doctoral training and had first become a committed birder. I had achieved my goals as Section Head of Pediatric Hematology-Oncology in Albany, and I had always wanted to return to Colorado.

I accepted the offer, arrived in Denver in December 1988, and settled into a new home in the foothills of the Rockies, southwest of town. I was soon back at work and reunited with several of my former professional colleagues. I had been away since 1974. I had returned to specialize in childhood brain tumors, which had not responded as well as other childhood cancers to modern therapy. Within four years, I would decide to leave pediatrics and focus on adults with brain cancer, since there were few, if any, specialists willing to take on this challenge. A neurosurgeon and I partnered to create a comprehensive adult program that I would lead for the remainder of my career, treating patients with the intent to cure them and sometimes succeeding.

During my earlier years in Denver, I had lived in the city, where there were a few parks, but little else of interest to a birder. Now I found myself in the relatively undisturbed environment of an old ranch in the foothills of the Rockies, converted into a residential enclave where the number of homes was limited to preserve the natural habitat of chaparral and mixed coniferous forest. Here, I often watched a pair of Golden Eagles flying overhead. They had a nest on top of the Lockheed Martin building a few miles away. I often stopped my car to watch these majestic raptors, which are found nearly everywhere in the Northern Hemisphere around the globe. I never saw anyone else doing the same thing, and I observed the same inattention by my neighbors when we were socializing. I was the outsider, but what is the price of fitting in?

You certainly don't need to be a birder to be awed by an eagle; at least that is what I thought to myself. I have always considered a day to be a good one if it included seeing an eagle, no matter what else transpired.

We birders call it bird blindness—the phenomenon of people not seeing birds, no matter how conspicuous. The problem usually goes beyond birds to other natural phenomena. This is not a medical diagnosis, but it does, I believe, deprive those who have it of many enriching experiences. I vividly recall once driving solo across the border from Colorado to New Mexico, headed for Santa Fe. I was listening to the spiritual song "Starwalker" by Buffy Sainte-Marie when a Golden Eagle soared across my field of vision. I was moved into a kind of reverie by the scenery, the majestic bird, and the music. I felt uniquely connected to the world. Moments like this cannot be orchestrated; they just happen if you are open to them, and more likely if you are alone.

If I had bird blindness, I would have missed this imprinted moment.

In my early days of birding in Colorado, I had located and observed some of the chicken-like gallinaceous species for which Colorado is a mecca for serious birders. Now during my second, longer stint, the gallinaceous sightings continued. The first of these occurred in a very unusual way. I was on call one weekend, making rounds at the hospital when I was summoned to one of the nursing stations and told that my second wife, Julie, was on the phone. She seldom called when I was seeing patients. We had two small children by then, my only son Robin, and my third daughter, Patty, so I was concerned that something was wrong.

"What's going on?" I asked.

"There's a really strange bird outside," Julie said, "sitting in our whiskey-barrel planter."

I could hear the excitement in her voice. I tried to disguise my suspicion that I had been unnecessarily interrupted. "What does it look like?"

"It's a dark bird with a small head and a plump body," she said.

"Sounds like a pigeon," I replied dismissively. "I'll check it when I get home if it's still there."

I arrived home an hour or two later. By then, the bird was on the roof of our house. I got a good look before it flew to the ground and slowly walked into the open space behind the house, where it disappeared, no doubt on its way back to the forest where it belonged.

It was a Blue Grouse.

Certainly no pigeon, the Blue Grouse—now called a Dusky— is one of the most difficult species of gallinaceous birds to find, since unlike Prairie Chickens and other gallinaceous species, they do not predictably gather to mate every year in the same place. The Dusky Grouse is usually found only by chance in its preferred montane habitat, or perhaps on your roof in the suburbs.

 *The species was split into the Dusky, which lives in the Rockies, and the Sooty, which lives in the Sierras and Alaska.*

I sheepishly "ate crow" and admitted to Julie with humility that she had found a truly great bird. I had no idea why it was in our yard and never saw it there again. From that day forward, I never ignored any bird observations Julie made. Her sharp eyes later spotted a Little Gull in the Bay of Fundy near Campobello Island, New Brunswick, the only one I have ever seen.

When the kids were of early school age, I thought they would enjoy a birding adventure. Julie was a good sport, so we planned a trip in early spring to a remote area of southeastern Colorado in search of the critically endangered Lesser Prairie Chicken.

I had seen the Greater years before with Michael Linshaw. At the time of this writing, the Lesser Prairie Chicken is essentially extinct in Colorado. The birding tours that target Colorado's many species of gallinaceous birds must go into Kansas to find them.

Colorado's last Lesser Prairie Chickens were confined to a single lek in an area near Springfield, Colorado, a remote place called Campo in the southeast corner of the state.

On the way from Denver in search of the Lesser Prairie Chicken, I was pulled over in the middle of nowhere on a lonely road by a State Highway Patrol Officer who had timed my vehicle's speed at about 90 mph (144 km/h).

"What's your hurry?" he said, after the customary long, slow walk to the car.

"I have to get to Campo in time to see Lesser Prairie Chickens before sundown," I said with a bit of desperation in my voice.

"What are Prairie Chickens?" he inquired.

"The Lesser Prairie Chicken," I said. "It's a rare bird seen in Colorado near Springfield. Nearly extinct."

I glanced at Julie and the kids. They were frozen by the drama.

The officer looked dumbfounded and asked, "Do you have a photo?"

I showed him my field guide, which confirmed my story and showed paintings of the bird and its distribution. He was fascinated by my description of the chicken and was shocked that he had never heard of something so unusual in his neck of the woods.

"Good luck and slow down," he said, and did not issue a ticket.

My family had become a bit agitated by the law-enforcement encounter, but quickly recovered their enthusiasm for the adventure. They were accustomed to my birding escapades, but a night in the Springfield slammer might have been over the top.

We arrived in rural and nondescript Springfield, found our motel, and hurried to the lek site about 25 miles from the town,

Springfield, Colorado Town Hall - Jail in Rear

reached via a series of numbered dirt roads. The site itself is so remote that we could not see any sign of humans or human activity, other than the road itself—no fences, signs, or telephone poles. We parked near the lek, as we had been instructed to do by the local game and wildlife ranger, and waited in silence. As the light faded, we started to hear clucking, which was soon followed by the birds arriving one at a time, ostensibly from nowhere. The males began their primal dance as the purplish tissue on their necks pulsated as if they were dancing to disco music. The females, predictably, paid no attention but wandered coquettishly about, just as the Greater Prairie Chicken hens had done years before.

Soon it was dark, and the birds had vanished. We miraculously found our way back to town guided by the brilliant stars and planets (still no GPS in those days) and turned in for the night. We were satisfied that we had witnessed something uniquely wild and fragile; moreover, we had not intruded. What I told the police officer about the bird's likely extinction in Colorado has, regrettably, come true.

In retrospect, this experience was one of the most meaningful in my long list of meaningful birding experiences because I was able to share it with my second litter of young children and their mom. I believe they understood this then and still do. The shameless public mating of the birds, however, did elicit demands for "the big talk" from both kids, which Julie and I, of course, failed to provide.

A few years later, after the Gunnison Sage Grouse was split from the Greater Sage Grouse into a new species, I was able to see it in early spring displaying near—you guessed it—Gunnison, Colorado, near the Gunnison River. The birds could be viewed from

Lesser Prairie Chicken

Gunnison Sage Grouse

a small parking area located on a dirt road that led to a hot springs resort. That seemed like a taunt, considering the frigid weather. It was necessary to arrive before dawn and remain in the car until the dancing birds disappeared. Julie and I drove to Gunnison the night before and stayed in a motel, then we arose about 4 a.m. to get to the spot in time. Gunnison is arguably the coldest place in Colorado, and that morning was no exception.

Once parked at the observation point, it was illegal to run the car, so we had no heat during the two-plus hours we were there. To use my scope, I had to keep the window open. The good news was that the birds arrived as predicted, danced their dance, and flew away. We could see the characteristic dark head, tiny bill, white breast, and the erect fan of striped tail feathers. I shivered my way back to Denver, about four hours away, with a new, rare, and endangered bird on my life list. I finally got a good look at a sage grouse, but not the Greater Sage Grouse, which is still called Greater even though there is still no lesser. At least it finally has something to be greater than.

With the addition of the Gunnison Sage Grouse to my life list, I had seen all of the coveted gallinaceous birds of Colorado. By itself, that is an accomplishment, but the adventures I had in the process were indelible and included family members and the friend who started the whole thing, Michael Linshaw. Over many miles of driving, running, biking, hiking, climbing, and birding, I had explored parts of Colorado—a place of magnificent beauty and diversity—that I never would have seen otherwise.

Still, my time there had been equally characterized by the trademark ups and downs of the birding life: sometimes puzzling, other times maddening, always exhilarating.

In 2015, after returning to Denver from a holiday in Cape Breton, I discovered that I had missed an opportunity to see a Barnacle Goose, which was being seen just minutes from the highway that took us from Cape Breton to the airport in Halifax. For years, I had been looking for an opportunity to see this rare goose, which strays from Greenland and northern Europe. It is seen nearly annually somewhere along the northeastern coast of North America but tends to disappear quickly.

As I was bemoaning my bad luck with the goose, reports appeared on the Internet of another rare goose that I hadn't seen, a Pink-footed Goose, which was found on a pond only miles from my loft in downtown Denver. It had never been seen in Colorado before. I was at the pond at daybreak the next morning and soon found the bird, which was close enough to see well. It was quite content, standing out in a large flock of Canada Geese.

Within a few days, there was another report, again very close to home, this time in Longmont, Colorado, of a Fork-tailed Flycatcher. This bird is common in Central and South America, and I had seen one briefly in Argentina. It appears at least once a year in the United States but disappears quickly. It is more commonly seen by birders who have the wherewithal to drop everything and chase the bird, wherever it might be, at a moment's notice. I was lucky and found the bird easily by driving to the site and simply going to where there were birders with their scopes and cameras trained on it. Majestic Longs Peak, one of Colorado's iconic Fourteeners, was in the background as I gazed at this rare and spectacular bird that had decided, inexplicably, to be the first of its kind to spend a day in Colorado. I aimed my glasses at the spot and focused on a black and white bird with a relatively small body and an outrageously long forked tail that moved gracefully when it flew. Thus, I had seen two extraordinary and unexpected life birds within minutes of my home, after cluelessly missing a Barnacle Goose on my way home from Nova Scotia.

Shortly thereafter, I was shocked to learn that a Barnacle Goose appeared in a pond not far from another pond where I had seen the Pink-footed Goose. It might have been the same goose that I missed in Nova Scotia! I rushed to see it before work early in the morning and was told by several birders that it had been present but had just flown away. I returned after work and aggressively navigated a logjam of commuters to get there quickly. Once again, I missed the goose by just minutes. That was it. The bird disappeared and hasn't been seen in Colorado since that brief appearance.

Fork-tailed Flycatcher   Pink-footed Goose

How do I explain the unlikelihood of all of these extraordinary birding events happening at all, let alone within days of each other? The answer is that I can't explain it. I felt like I was being teased, but by whom? Unusual events and situations beg an explanation, and many people are so desperate to have one that they will believe just about anything that suits their need. I must simply conclude that my crazy experience described above was, as Walter Cronkite would have said, just "the way it is."

While I may envy those who believe in some sort of Providence, my spirituality comes from being dazzled by beauty, love, and work. My bird sightings require direct and careful observation, and that is where I find my comfort. Some philosopher once said, "I think, therefore I am."

PART 4

PEREGRINATIONS

ARIZONA:
MY FIRST EXPEDITIONS TO A BIRDER'S PARADISE

RULE 9
Individual goals are seldom accomplished
without the assistance of others.

Arizona, particularly southeastern Arizona, with the city of Tucson as its hub, is blessed with a unique geography consisting of several towering mountain ranges divided by low desert basins. The mountains tend to extend from northwest to southeast and from the southern edge of other similar formations farther north. Each of the ranges has unique features, which include significant differences in habitat for wildlife, especially birds. For serious birders, several of these mountainous areas are iconic and feature many sought-after bird species, which include regular nesters and less predictable accidentals.

The musical names of these ranges are the Santa Ritas, Huachucas, Santa Catalinas, Galluros, Patagonias, Pimalenos,

Accidental: a species found where it is not expected to be, also called a vagrant. This phenomenon also occurs among humans, often with unfortunate consequences.

Chiracahuas, Santa Teresas, Tumacacons, Pajaritos, and the Pelloncillos, which extend into New Mexico.

Between the mountain ranges, which rise steeply from the intervening basins, are areas of desert full of canyons, gulches, washes, and other hotspots where unique habitats are created by transitions between the elements described above. The famous Patagonia road stop is one of these. Others, (to name only a few), include Ramsey Canyon, Madera Canyon, California Gulch, Patagonia Lake, and Florida Wash. Of course, all of these areas are close to the Mexican border, where birds from more tropical areas often stray north to be found by the plethora of skilled birders who prowl these productive areas.

In addition to birds, this region features other wildlife of interest, such as javelinas, coatimundis, Gila monsters, and the odd jaguar. The plant life is spectacular, especially when there has been rain. Within hours, the desert can turn into a Garden of Eden, filled with colors and shapes that are especially arresting for those who don't live there. The rain tends to come in monsoons, which can be violent and often cause flash flooding. The city of Tucson has numerous canals to divert water from the roads to prevent these biblical downpours from causing danger and inconvenience. The climate is arid, but very salubrious when the heat is not at its peak, which can reach 120°F.

I made my first trip to this region, armed with the *Lane Field Guide to the Birds of Arizona*, during my period of pediatric training in Denver between 1971 and 1974. I drove down in an old Volvo with Jim McCorkle, an Alaskan whom I had met on field trips of the Denver Field Ornithologists. He was a crusty character, a loner, but very competent to manage the necessities of camping in the desert, which we, with our very limited budget, had resolved to do.

This trip was marred by a series of relatively minor mishaps that added up. First, my binoculars somehow became damaged so that I could see clearly only with one eye. My birding skills were in a developmental stage, so this was a significant hindrance. Next, the front windshield of the Volvo sedan came loose in a gust of wind. We had no opportunity to repair it, so, for the rest of the trip, we had wind and dust blowing in our faces whenever the car was moving. To distract ourselves, we drank outrageous quantities of Dr Pepper, which seemed to help; perhaps the caffeine and sugar high was the explanation, but I have avoided that drink ever since.

We made the long drive from Denver to southwestern New Mexico on the first day and camped along the road, hearing whip-poor-wills as we fell asleep in our tent.

At that time, we didn't know that we were listening to Mexican Whip-poor-wills, which appear identical to what is now the Eastern Whip-poor-will but have a noticeably different call.

The next day, we made it to our first destination, Guadalupe Canyon, a remote area that lies on the Mexican border and straddles the New Mexico/Arizona border. It is about 30 miles from Douglas, Arizona, the nearest town. A stream flows through the meandering canyon, which is lined with sycamores and cottonwoods. The canyon walls are steep, and the rock has an unusual and very striking rose color. Ranchers along the canyon made the area available for visiting birders and others interested in this unique place.

The canyon had once been a favorite sanctuary for the Apache and Chiricahua tribes of Native Americans led by Chief Geronimo. It is home to several varieties of birds that are scarce and local. These include Thick-billed Kingbirds, Varied Bunting, Buff-collared Nightjar, and Zone-tailed Hawk, among others. It is also a place in which unusual and threatened mammals such as the ocelot, coatimundi, and even the rare jaguar can find refuge. Sadly, President Donald Trump designated this canyon as a site on which to build one of his ignominious walls. The wall, as expected, has turned a remote and cherished place into an eyesore where the movement of rare wildlife has been negatively altered.

Fortunately, our visit preceded Trump by several decades, and we were able to camp in the canyon in its original primitive condition. It was there that I saw my first Thick-billed Kingbird, which awakened us with its strident call early in the morning. I raced out of the tent to get a look and stayed away long enough for Jim to make the coffee, something that put a bit of a strain on our already tenuous relationship, although I had never asked him to make coffee. I was there for the birds, perhaps to a fault. We also found a Zone-tailed Hawk on its nest, and I saw my first Varied Bunting, though not very well with one eye through my damaged binoculars.

From Guadalupe Canyon in the Peloncillo Mountains, we drove to Cave Creek Canyon in the next range west—the Chiricahuas. Unfortunately, drought conditions were in effect, with a high risk of fire. This prevented us from exploring the Chiricahuas and the meandering and productive road through them, which ascends to Rustler's Park, the territory of Mexican Chickadees, Olive Warblers, and Yellow-eyed Juncos.

It also radically reduced our chances of finding an Elegant Trogon, known at that time as the Coppery-tailed Trogon. This bird was at the top of our target list for the trip.

Nevertheless, we had an evening full of Western Screech Owls and marauding javelinas, pig-like animals that are genetically related to elephants. These feisty beasts were fearless and traipsed through our campsite as if we weren't there. They had a strong, musty odor that announced their presence and lingered after they had departed. This experience reminded me, for some reason, of some relatives who stayed too long.

Our next stop was Patagonia near the town of Nogales, a major border crossing town due south of Tucson. At the time, Patagonia was a hotspot where many rare birds had been found at an otherwise undistinguished roadside rest stop. We were able to find someone locally to help us locate a few birds, including a Rose-throated Becard, a flycatcher with a striking rosy spot in the throat of the male. We were also able to find a Five-striped Sparrow, one of the first identified in North America, by climbing a thorny embankment that resulted in a few scrapes, thorn punctures, and some strong language. The bird, found singing peacefully at the top of the cliff, was very handsome, with white stripes on the head and throat against a grey background. Its song is the closest of all birds I have heard to saying "tweet tweet." After the unpleasant and bloody climb to find it, this "song" made me laugh, which abruptly silenced the offended bird.

These were the highlights of my first of many forays into the birders' paradise of southeastern Arizona.

In 1988, once again living in Colorado, I would finally have more opportunities to return to Arizona to see its resident specialty birds and chase rarities. These opportunities would, by necessity, be short and infrequent, consumed as I was with work and family responsibilities, but I gradually accumulated a respectable list of lifers.

Lifer: A species of bird seen for the first time in a birder's life, not necessarily the bird's life.

This is an iconic event for birders and of such great importance that it can challenge the judgment (and honesty) of any birder. Thus, photography (un-doctored), which I took up late in my career as a birder, is arguably the surest way to be certain that a bird has been seen. As with much of life, there is no absolute certainty, especially with the odd birder (redundancy) who is afflicted with voluntary hallucinations. I was setting the stage for an unexpected quest, thirty-two years later, to achieve the birder's Holy Grail: seeing 800 species in North America.

The USA, Canada, and Hawaii as defined by the American Birding Association (ABA). Mexico, which is part of everyone else's definition of North America, is excluded; after all, the ABA is a covey of birders.

The first thing I did was book Bob Buttery to guide me. He was an active and skilled Colorado birder when I first joined the Denver Field Ornithologists in the early 1970s. Now nearly twenty years later, he had moved to southeastern Arizona for retirement, but did some bird guiding. I booked him for a few days to look for an Elegant Trogon and a Rufous-capped Warbler, a rarity that was being seen in French Joe Canyon in the Chiricahua Mountains. We went for the warbler first, driving from Tucson to French Joe Canyon, which is inadequately birded due to its limited accessibility. The canyon has a small stream and is impassible to cars. Vehicles must be parked at the entrance. But someone had found this secretive warbler while hiking and listening along the stream bed.

Cap (crown): That part of a bird from which a tuft extends— if the bird has a tuft—or where the bird sports a kippah if Jewish, a sombrero if Mexican, or a beanie if pledged to a fraternity.

Accordingly, we hiked and listened, but without any evidence of our bird—until we encountered another birder who had found the warbler and volunteered to show us the spot.

Most birders are generous and empathetic toward kindred bird seekers, while a few rotten apples will go to extremes to out-bird others.

We got to the spot but had difficulty raising the skulking bird from its cover along the stream bed. Exasperated, I took a break and walked into the bushes to relieve myself. The sound of "running water" got the attention of the bird, and he popped out of the brush and into view. I was, as it were, stuck where I stood, with only one free hand to manage my binocs. I got a brief look at this imposing and very rare bird, with its orange cap and face framed by a green back and yellow throat, before it returned to the protection of the thick flora. My colleagues, both of whom had better views than I, had a good laugh. Of course, I took credit for the sighting since the sound of running water often attracts birds. Many birders make a "pishing" sound (with their mouths) as a means of inducing reluctant birds to reveal themselves.

Pishing: a noise like running water made by birders to attract birds, which annoys and alarms most non-birders enough to keep them away.

Elated by our success, we traveled next to Cave Creek Canyon to look for an Elegant Trogon. This bird is emblematic of the avian fauna of southeastern Arizona. It looks parrot-like, but has a small head and is, unlike the gregarious parrots and allies, solitary and reclusive. It belongs to a large family of birds, Trogoniformes, found in Central and South America, and among the most colorful and diverse bird families. In the United States, this bird is found exclusively in canyons close to the Mexican border, where it tends to feed by moving up and down stream beds. This makes it hard to find, though when present, it is readily identified by its primitive barking call. The bird was high on my most-wanted list. I had missed it on my

Elegant Trogon

first visit years earlier with Jim McCorkle, when the canyons were closed by a high risk of fire.

Bob and I arrived and had the canyon to ourselves. We didn't hear or see the bird but decided to exercise patience and wait in the general area where it had been reported, with the expectation that it would eventually return. In about an hour, we heard the call. I could feel my heart pounding as was nearly always the case when I confidently anticipated seeing a coveted new bird. Soon, we spotted our bird perched in good view in a sycamore tree. It boasted a brilliant crimson breast and underparts topped by a narrow white stripe. The head was iridescent green, and the bill was bright yellow. The eye had a yellow eye-ring, and the narrow, spotted tail was about as long as the body. It had some buffy coloration on the upper tail—which is why the species used to be called the Coppery-tailed Trogon.

Everything about this bird says *primitive, tropical, surreal*. Seeing it was a thrill, and I will be just as thrilled if I ever see another.

Unfortunately, Bob wasn't feeling well by the time we saw this "elegant" wonder. He had some gastrointestinal bug or perhaps had eaten some desert sushi, who knows. He was eating only applesauce and saltines. He asked if there was anything else I wanted to see, but we had accomplished our goals. It was time for his day to end.

There is always a fine line with a guide and how hard to push. I have learned to be gentler as I have aged and, I hope, matured. Bird guiding might sound romantic, but it is hard work, with customers who can be demanding and sometimes unappreciative. I have great respect for the good ones, and I have had several, including Bob Buttery, the man who helped me find my first trogon.

Flame-colored Tanager
Photograph by Dr. David MacDonald

FLAME-COLORED TANAGER IN MADERA CANYON

RULE 10
No fence is strong enough or high enough
to withstand human kindness.

In early spring, about 2006, a Flame-colored Tanager, a Mexican and Central American bird of the most brilliant red-orange imaginable, appeared in Madera Canyon in the Santa Rita Mountains south of Tucson. The early mornings were quite chilly when the bird made its daily appearance, and as parking was not allowed in the area, a bit of a climb up the canyon road was necessary, which worsened the chill after working up a sweat.

When I arrived at the site, there was already a small gathering of intrepid birders garbed in the usual formless but functional attire. As I recall, we were near the famous Santa Rita Lodge, with its many hummingbird feeders and legendary sightings. There were very few birds around, other than the always flamboyant Painted Redstarts and a few resident hummers. We waited quite a while, shivering and apprehensive about missing the tanager. Finally, the bird appeared. It was as if we had witnessed the Christmas tree lighting in New York City. Suddenly, this splotch of orange-red perched in a tree turned a damp and dreary morning into a celebration of light and color.

As I drove at a leisurely pace back to my lodging, contemplating what I had just seen, I encountered a random Border

Patrol roadblock. It occurred to me, as I answered the routine monotone questions, that the bird I was so grateful to have seen was certainly from Mexico and had crossed the border for its own good reasons, without either realizing there was a border or giving a hoot. Troubled by these discordant thoughts, I wrote this poem:

Border Patrol

Strangely dressed people bearing binoculars
shiver in the morning gloom of
Madera Canyon in Arizona's
Santa Rita Mountains.
They huddle and wait for
a Flame-colored Tanager
the only one in North America
a startling bird orange-on-orange.
A few miles away is the Mexican border
where one step changes everything.
The poor step north looking for work.
The rich step south to escape it
but birds don't have borders
these neotropical gems
sought by birders
who lust to see them
on "their" side of the border.
Nearby lurk the Border Patrol.
Not seekers of birds
it's people they hunt
harmless as the tanager.
Immigrant-bred patriots rant as
the Statue of Liberty
grounded
stands tall
impervious to wind.

Edward Arenson MD, circa 2006

"Give me your tired, your poor, your huddled masses yearning to breathe free, the wretched refuse of your teeming shore."
- Emma Lazarus, Jewish immigrant, 1883.

"Mr. Gorbachev, tear down that wall!"
- President Ronald Reagan, Berlin, 1987

"Blessed are the merciful, for they will be shown mercy."
- Jesus, the Beatitudes, C.E. 0033.

Buff–collared Nightjar

Montezuma Quail - Photograph
Provided by Melody Kehl

A HEAD-RAISING JOURNEY TO CALIFORNIA GULCH

I have birded in southeastern Arizona numerous times, and always find something new and exciting. I have also enjoyed the knowledge, expertise, and company of several of the finest birding guides to be found anywhere. Among these are Bob Buttery, Rick Wright, and Melody Kehl. Yet despite all these trips and several excursions to locations where Montezuma Quail might be seen, by 2014—after 42 years of birding—I'd still never seen one.

Birders use the term "nemesis bird" to describe this kind of frustrating experience. Many birders and guides had told me, as if it were any consolation, that this elusive but handsome bird is "usually found when you're not looking for it." In a way, it is like love, which is most often found unexpectedly rather than when it is sought. It is important, however, to be aware when you are in a good place to find the quail. The same is true for love. California Gulch would not be a good place to go looking for love, but it is a place where these elusive quail might be found. Let me explain.

That year, a Buff-collared Nightjar was being seen regularly in California Gulch.

Nightjars are strange birds with amorphous bodies. Most are nocturnal. Common examples of North American nightjars are Whip-poor-wills, Common and Lesser Nighthawks, and Chuck-will's-widows, which I had in my yard in Georgia.

I had never seen a Buff-collared Nightjar either, nor had I ever been to California Gulch, so I contacted Melody Kehl and arranged to try for this rare bird with her and a few other stalwart birders.

Melody wisely waited until she had assembled a group to minimize the number of trips to the Gulch, which has good birds but is one of the most inhospitable places imaginable. We were accompanied by her faithful and more than patient husband, Eric (of blessed memory), who packed a formidable pistol, a necessity in this remote area which is a favored route for "coyotes," smugglers of drugs across the border from Mexico. Since there is no easy way in or out of the Gulch, it is best to be vigilant and prepared.

This renowned birding hotspot is located about 20 miles west of the Arizona border town of Nogales, which is an hour south of Tucson. Once you turn off the highway and head west, the road becomes increasingly hazardous to navigate. Melody and Eric collected the group, and our journey began. I noticed a pile of folding chairs and a large cooler in the back of Melody's SUV. We were all jovial and happy to be fed some coffee and muffins by our guide. Everything went smoothly as we traveled south from our inn in Tucson.

Once we made the turn west toward the gulch, the journey became less and less pleasant. The road deteriorated into a track with numerous hazards like rocks, fallen foliage, and bumps that were sufficient to make us temporarily weightless and tested the strength of our seatbelts. It took us about two hours to navigate the 20 miles into the Gulch, which runs more or less north and south and is sometimes flooded after heavy rains. As we got deeper into the wilderness, we began to see abandoned campsites with scattered refuse and spent fires. These had been left by people crossing the border at night. Some of these were certainly the infamous and very dangerous "coyotes" while others were harmless refugees seeking work in the United States. The long, uncomfortable journey and the signs of danger gave us a sense of uneasiness and queasy stomachs as we approached our destination.

After what seemed like several hours of uncomfortable travel, we parked in an open area with evidence of recent habitation by humans. This was where we would try to locate the Nightjar, but not until dusk. We unloaded the chairs and the cooler and prepared to spend a few hours birding deeper in the Gulch until it was time to enjoy our meal and prepare for the arrival of the nocturnal bird.

First, however, since I had announced that the Montezuma Quail was a nemesis bird for me, Melody suggested a casual walk around the clearing into the surrounding brush. She instructed us to keep our eyes trained ahead about ten to fifteen yards as we walked. Most people are inclined to watch the ground closer to their feet, which is optimal for preventing a fall but not helpful for locating birds that stay on the ground at a safe distance from any perceived threat. This is where a guide, if your experience and skills are limited like mine, is crucial. Melody thought she might have heard some clucking, and there were quail tracks everywhere on the dusty ground. Not more than five minutes passed before we spotted these beautifully marked quail. They have a black and white clown's face, while polka-dots glorify the belly. Once we found the first quail and knew where to look, we saw many more. As you might imagine, I was elated, and all the previous frustrations and hours of searching unsuccessfully for this bird were erased in an instant. The others were equally pleased to spot this difficult bird. I believe Melody knew we would find the quail but was too astute to promise.

After some birding in the lower canyon where we saw some border specialties, we returned to the clearing where Melody's husband Eric stood guard, silently brandishing his 9mm pistol in full view. Melody arranged the chairs in a semicircle as we waited for the sun to drop below the horizon. She instructed us to be silent, listen for the bird, attempt to locate it by triangulation of sound, then shine our flashlights and, hopefully, get a glimpse.

The calls started on cue in the twilight. We were serenaded by a staccato repetition of *cu cu cuc cuc oh chee* sounds echoing out of the darkness. The calls got progressively louder and closer, finally localizing in the bushes near our feet. Melody pointed, and we aimed our lights. We found the Buff-collared Nightjar perched low in the brush, its huge retinas brilliant red in our flashlight beams, and then it vanished. With the flashlights shining, I could see the toothy grins of the covey of thrilled birders.

This technique is yet another ingenious approach, known by some guides and expert birders, to finding difficult birds. It dramatically increases the chance of success. Another example is driving a car very slowly, headlights dimmed, along dirt roads while looking for the red retinal reflection in a bird's eyes.

Having found the Nightjar, we did some hearty high-fives and back pats, gave well-deserved kudos to our leader, and began the long and arduous journey back to Tucson. We arrived exhausted but safe, sound, and fulfilled. I swore to myself I would never return to that remote and dangerous place. But, as you should know by now, that oath could be violated at any time by the arrival of one of the miraculous birds that regularly appear in this desolate border country.

A NOCTURNAL TREK FOR A TUFTED FLYCATCHER

RULE 12
Many pleasurable things come with pain,
but don't let the pain prevent the pleasure.

In June of 2016, I learned of a bonanza of rare birds in southeast Arizona. There were reports of regular sightings of Tufted Flycatchers, a real rarity, even in this land of rarities, in Carr Canyon. At the same time, the first Pine Flycatcher north of Mexico was being seen in the Santa Rita Mountains at an out-of-the-way campsite in Garden Canyon, not frequented by birders because of its terrible access road. Finally, a pair of rare Slate-throated Redstarts were nesting right off the road in the Chiricahua Mountains. This is the kind of situation I am constantly hoping for: multiple new birds in a single foray. Of course, there is always some factor that makes things difficult. In this case, it was the heat from the "fake news" of global climate change. The peak temperature was predicted to be about 120°F.

To reduce the danger of dehydration in this remote canyon, my trusty guide, Melody Kehl, who had kept us safe during our trip to California Gulch, rightly insisted on carrying a huge load of water. She had been unjustly criticized when one of her clients was noncompliant and became so dehydrated that he had to be rescued and hospitalized. This was a challenge for me because I, like many men in their 70s, had some degree of prostate enlargement and needed to relieve myself frequently. Fortunately, we were in the woods where the trees provided some privacy; nonetheless, it was a bit embarrassing for me, though Melody had encountered this phenomenon many times before and thought nothing of it.

To minimize our heat exposure, we started about 4 a.m. Melody brought coffee and pastries, and we made a beeline for Carr Canyon and arrived in the dark. The steep, winding road was unlit and deserted. It felt like we were dreaming and, given the hour, we should have been. As we ascended in our SUV, we were delighted to see the nocturnal Mexican Whip-poor-will, my first sighting since it was split from the Eastern Whip-poor-will, and a Whiskered Screech Owl highlighted in the headlight beams.

Mexican Whip-poor-will

Tufted Flycatcher - Photograph
Provided by Melody Kehl

We were dropped off by Eric, who would meet us hours later in Ramsey Canyon. We set out with headlamps in cool temperatures on our trek of several miles, taking care not to trip and fall. At sun-up, we arrived at the sight of the Tufted Flycatchers.

Tuft: A silly triangular point of feathers on the crown of certain birds that resembles some unfortunate hairdo choices I often refer to as hair-don'ts.

We waited for the birds to become active, which did not take long. They were darting to and from the same tree, which helped us locate their nesting site. We had plenty of time to observe their characteristic pointed tufts, buffy faces, and buffy bellies. To my knowledge, we had found the first nest of this species in North America. We were soon joined by some other birders, including a father and son, who shared our joy and reward for our efforts.

We trekked out through Ramsey Canyon, where we met Eric, who had shuttled the SUV. As we walked through this iconic birding hotspot, Melody told me stories about its past history of birding glory and more recent and unfortunate decline since its acquisition by the Nature Conservancy. The near-complete lack of bird activity or song was obvious. We saw unnecessary signs and fences, mulched trails, and other forms of tampering with something that was just fine the way it was. Melody showed me the site of a previously threatened species of frog, now totally absent, but luckily discovered in some

Sunrise in Carr Canyon

Morning in Carr Canyon

other "unimproved" location. Once out of Ramsey, we beat the heat back to our motel, where I ventured a swim, but found the water warm enough to poach an egg. Instead I retreated to my air-conditioned room.

The next day, we traveled first to the site of the Pine Flycatcher, Aliso Springs in Gardner Canyon.

This is one of several flycatchers in the genus Empidonax. These flycatchers are small, prone to move frequently as they hunt for insects, and very difficult to distinguish from one another by sight.

This was the first and only Pine Flycatcher to be recorded north of Mexico, although there had been other unconfirmed reports. This flycatcher was discovered on May 28, 2016, by Dave Stejskal, who noticed that it was making a nest that would be uncharacteristic for any other Empidonax in the dry oak/pine habitat. Its sharp "whit" call was also inconsistent with any known nesting species in the area. He was so excited that he summoned an expert from the Midwest who came and verified his discovery.

We were warned that the road to the campground was quite treacherous, and one spot was so steep we would need to get out of the vehicle while Melody's husband gunned the engine to prevent stopping. If he stopped, the vehicle would never make it, and we would be forced to walk several steep miles in the stifling sun. Before we started our adventure up this road, we were taking a break for some water and a snack when we were serenaded by an exuberant trill coming from the trees.

I didn't recognize the song and asked Melody what it was. "Botteri's Sparrow," she replied nonchalantly. This relatively nondescript sparrow is a much-coveted bird that I had seen just once in winter but had never heard. I was excited, since hearing a bird sing greatly enhances the experience of finding it. People usually think of birding as a visual experience, but in many cases, as with the Botteri's Sparrow (rare and local but visually bland), the song is quintessential. I already had this bird on my life list, but hearing its song for the first time made it feel like a lifer all over again.

The trip up the road turned out to be quite enjoyable. Melody knew the campground was occupied and we must not disturb the campers at such an early hour. Fortunately, we were able to spot the Pine Flycatcher from the periphery in the trees directly over the tents before it landed on the ground of the open campsite, where we got a good, but very brief look. This is not an easily identified bird, but we could hear its diagnostic song, which is triphasic and complemented by a sharp *whit* repeated regularly. We all agreed to move on to the Chiricahua Mountains while the day was young and before the heat fell upon us. The Pine Flycatcher did make a nest and was present until it disappeared in July, having been seen by hundreds of birders. Its closest known nesting area is a hundred miles south in western Mexico.

The ride from the Santa Ritas to the Chiricahuas is not short, but we managed to arrive relatively early, thanks to Melody's military, but necessary, schedule. As we ascended, we arrived where the Slate-throated Redstarts had been reported. We found them immediately after parking the car. The adult bird displayed its red cap and belly, black face, and slaty grey body. What we didn't expect to see were three chicks, not previously seen. Mouths agape, we watched them follow a parent across the road into a streambed. These were the first chicks of this accidental species ever photographed in North America. We were lucky because, once chicks are fledged, the birds become silent and disappear. Melody, usually composed, was so excited that she called a friend and insisted she drive to the site immediately.

Our day was complete, and we were able to avoid the extreme heat, but we were exhausted by the time we returned to Tucson. No exhaustion feels better than this—getting up at an ungodly hour, driving for hours to remote and dicey locations, and finding

Pine Flycatcher
Photograph Provided by Melody Kehl

Slate-throated Redstart
Photograph Provided by Melody Kehl

Note the Pine Flycatcher's long tail, pointed eye ring, orange mandible, and absence of yellow in the throat.

rare birds and other natural sights. This day's accomplishments felt much the same as crossing the finish line of a marathon or a hundred-mile bike ride— the pain of success.

FLORIDA: THE DRY TORTUGAS

When my parents were living in Florida in the early 1990s, I decided to visit them and take the opportunity to join a group birding trip to the Dry Tortugas.

The Dry Tortugas are part of the Florida Keys, extending many miles from Key West into Florida Bay. They are a prime stone crab habitat, and they provide opportunity to find a variety of seabirds that are rare on the mainland. In spring, these islands are a rest stop for a multitude of birds migrating north across the Gulf of Mexico. During earlier visits, I had managed to find some difficult birds on my own in the Palm Beach area, including Limpkin, Smooth-billed Ani, and Snail Kite, which I found at Loxahatchee Refuge by arriving before dawn when the birds were still roosting before their daily search for snails.

Our tour was organized by Wellington Biggins, an excellent birder and a bit of a character. An overnight boat ride from Key West would be required to reach Garden Key, an old fortress that was used to control pirates in the 19th century.

Before boarding our sturdy New England vessel, the Yankee Clipper (which was inexplicably in Florida) we spent the day birding our way from Miami to Key West. While we did see a few birds of interest, we missed a Stripe-headed Tanager in Miami (now called Western Spindalis) and failed to locate a Mangrove Cuckoo or an Antillean Nighthawk, which can be found at dusk at the airport on Marathon Key. The tanager had been found by a feisty group of women birders from Oklahoma City who were part of our tour group and reported their sighting before our tour began. Finding these three missed birds would require two additional Florida excursions and many years.

We departed, and I soon found myself in a hammock in a cabin about the size of a telephone booth with four other men. Our cabin was wedged into the wedge-shaped bow. Thanks to a powerful air conditioner and some Valium, I managed to sleep until I was awakened at dawn by a beam of light shining through the single

Snail Kite

Black Noddy Tern

porthole. I rose instantly and headed for the deck, where I was greeted on the horizon by the skyline of Garden Key and the ruins of the old fortress.

Birds were everywhere, various terns and Great Frigatebirds following the boat toward the dock. I wisely grabbed a quick hot shower, available only on deck, before being joined by the others. We spent the rest of the morning inside the old fort walls, where there is a fountain that drips fresh water continuously. I sat and watched a menagerie of exhausted migratory birds literally walking over our feet as they sipped water from the fountain and foraged for food. We saw many birds this way, rather than how they are ordinarily seen, in the crowns of towering trees or partially hidden in lush foliage. I made the mistake of going outside the fortress to explore the surrounding bushes and missed a rare Bicknell's Thrush. The compulsion to explore can have its rewards, but it wasn't worth the risk of leaving the iconic fountain.

Impatience is not helpful for birding. It took me 24 years to see the bird I missed.

After lunch, we explored the nearby islands in an inflatable Zodiac and found a wonderful variety of seabirds, including two species of boobies—the Masked Booby and Brown Booby— and four species of terns—Sooty, Roseate, Brown Noddy, and the rare Black Noddy. After that, we snorkeled in pristine water around one of the small, protected islands, where I saw dozens of different tropical fish, corals, and other invertebrates. The whole day was a feast for the senses in perfect weather and warm, clear water.

That evening, we returned to the fort where we saw some nocturnal birds, including what was probably an Antillean Nighthawk, a target bird we might have seen in Marathon if we had simply waited for it to become active at dusk. It circled above us for at least an hour, but never uttered a sound, the only way it could be identified. Alas, it would take several years to add this species to my life list—at the risk of losing my marriage.

Later, I would conclude that this otherwise wonderful trip could have been even better if I had taken the time to identify the best leader, Larry Manfredi, about whom I will have much to say. We spent the rest of the evening exploring the moat that surrounds the fort with our flashlights. We found numerous nocturnal creatures at close range without the risk of being in the water, where we might have fed one of the nocturnal predators some fingers or toes.

And so ended an excellent, but imperfect, voyage to the Dry Tortugas. I had added seven birds to my life list in just over two days.

RULE 14
Aging is a challenge
accelerated by passivity.

Larry Manfredi and I had a great time eating and discussing a variety of topics; he is a well-educated Renaissance man who just happens to be a fellow birder and revered birding guide. A couple of Manhattans were consumed, a few lies told, and we made plans for the next day's birding. I asked him, expecting a negative response, if a Mangrove Cuckoo might be found within a reasonable distance. I believed this nemesis bird to be found exclusively in dense mangroves in the Keys and Everglades, where I had looked for it unsuccessfully many times. These birds are not rare but hard to localize and uncooperative to say the least. To my surprise, Larry said it might be possible to find one near Homestead, where I was staying and where he lives. I was dubious, but Larry is not the deceitful type and seemed confident.

The next morning, after a very welcome rest, we set out for a park in Homestead through which flowed a canal. It didn't look good to me. There were not many trees, and lots of people were present. Still, within a few minutes of skulking along the canal, we heard the loud squawks of the cuckoo. I stood, mouth agape, as the bird flew to an open perch where I did not even need to use my binoculars to see all of its striking field marks: orange mandible, pointed bill, and buffy underparts. This was my third life bird, so far, on this memorable trip.

Mandible: the lower part of the bill, found directly below the upper bill. Together, these form the pecker with which a bird, if it is a pecker, pecks.

It was December 2016, and there were at least two Western Spindalises present in the Miami area. A bird of the Caribbean that strays to Florida, it is the member of the tanager family I had missed on my trip to the Dry Tortugas about 25 years earlier. Of the two spotted in the Miami area, the male was seen only intermittently and

Mangrove Cuckoo
Photograph by Larry Manfredi

Female Western Spindalis
Photograph by Larry Manfredi

on private property, but the female was seen regularly in Bill Baggs Park in the vicinity of South Miami Beach.

The male Western Spindalis is more colorful than the female, often the case with birds, presumably for breeding purposes.

There was an early guided tour of the private area where it had been seen. I had a full workday on Friday but found a red-eye flight. I booked the flight with some ambivalence. I was 70 years old, not getting any younger, and phobic about sleep deprivation ever since my pediatric internship and its 36- hour shifts.

My red-eye flight arrived on time. My excellent guide, Larry Manfredi, collected me, and we went straight to the location of the guided walk for the male Western Spindalis, which we did not see. Instead, we got a magnificent view of a Short-tailed Hawk, an unexpected life bird. I also saw my first Scaly-breasted Munia, a bird I had never heard of—introduced to the region, but now breeding and therefore countable.

Having missed out on the male Western Spindalis, we headed next to Key Biscayne to look for the female at Bill Baggs Park. Although less colorful than the male, she is worthy of equal admiration. We heard and followed the Spindalis and got several brief looks, but she was not very accommodating. Ultimately, we were drenched by a sudden downpour and had to seek refuge before returning to the area,

 *Countable: An introduced bird that can be added to the birder's list if seen in a place where it breeds. The choice of locations like Texas and Miami should not be held against the birds that were clever enough to escape from human captors who brought them there without their permission.*

where we were overjoyed to confirm the identification. Feeling like our luck had turned, we got some fresh fish for lunch—one thing about Florida that I truly enjoy, as do many of its birds.

As we chatted, it dawned on me that I had just seen my 700th life bird! Larry agreed to join me that evening for a celebration at Joe's Stone Crab, an iconic institution in Miami Beach.

We headed on to Homestead, where I checked into my motel for a short rest and clean-up before Larry picked me up to head for Joe's. I hadn't slept in more than 36 hours, and I was operating on vapor and adrenaline.

Joe's Stone Crab is a venerable watering hole that has been in Miami Beach since the early 20th Century. It is known, oddly enough, for its stone crab claws. Stone crabs are found predominantly, but not exclusively, in the waters of Florida Bay. Once a crab is caught, one claw is removed and the crab is returned to the water, which allows the crab to survive and regenerate the missing claw. (I once naively explained this to a vegan friend who was horrified.) This treatment of the crabs has always appealed to my support for a self-sustaining food supply and, most importantly, allows me to enjoy the eating experience guilt-free.

As for the guilt, I must ignore my Jewish heritage when I eat this forbidden food. I have never really believed that God, who reputedly created the stone crab, would forbid his "chosen people" from eating something so delicious that lived halfway around the earth from the Sinai, where my ancestors, on foot without access to GPS, were ignominiously lost for 40 years. My mother, continuing the tradition years later, was living in Queens but was unable to find Kennedy Airport.

I had been to Joe's before in the company of my great-uncle Louis Arenson, Aunt Rose, and my parents, now all deceased. Since the place has never changed, I sensed the presence of these relatives who were early denizens of Miami Beach in days when Jews were denied access to many other restaurants and hotels in Florida. Another appeal of Joe's is that it has always offered very tasty but reasonably priced entrees, such as fried chicken and accouterments, to make sure that customers of limited means could eat there and eat well. There couldn't have been a better place to celebrate.

As we enjoyed our meal and each other's company, we discussed the dilemma of how to spend a few remaining hours the next day before I would need to get to the airport. In addition to the aforementioned Mangrove Cuckoo, Larry mentioned several now-listable birds that could be found in the area, all of them imports that had established breeding status. These included Egyptian Goose, Grey-headed Swamphen, and two species of parakeets.

We easily located these, except for the White-winged Parakeet, which we looked for while having lunch at yet another seafood restaurant. The bird never appeared, but the lunch was excellent. We also had the opportunity to explore old Miami, including the once and still fabulous Biltmore Hotel, where we found roosting Nanday Parakeets—another life bird. Larry dropped me at the airport, and I departed with the hope that I would get a chance to bird with him again soon.

Sure enough, about four months later in spring 2017, two rarities I had missed on my previous visit, the Thick-billed Vireo and La Sagra's Flycatcher, were found. I checked and found that the good old red-eye flight was available and called Larry to make sure he could guide me. I took the plunge (perhaps not the best terminology for air travel), and it paid off.

When I arrived, Larry told me that in addition to the rarities mentioned above, the White-winged Parakeet I had missed on my previous trip was now present. If I saw the rarities and this parakeet, I would add three new birds to my list. In addition, a Bananaquit had been reported in the same general area, though it had been only briefly seen. Because of the red-eye flight, I would have two full days to see these birds and anything else that turned up. Of course, taking this flight on Friday night after a full work week was going to be exhausting, but that's what it takes.

As soon as you begin to think of yourself as elderly, you are—and will soon suffer the consequences.

Larry had picked me up from the airport at 5:30 a.m. It was still dark, so we had breakfast at an IHOP as the sun rose. The IHOP was not chosen at random. After breakfast, we exited the parking lot with the windows open and soon heard the squawks of the promised White-winged Parakeets. We parked the car and found 10 or 15 birds

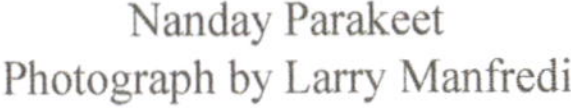

Nanday Parakeet
Photograph by Larry Manfredi

White-winged Parakeets
Photograph by Larry Manfredi

displaying spectacular white and yellow chevroned wings as they flew. They have white eye rings and pinkish bills, and are exceedingly handsome—my first life bird of the trip. It was obvious that Larry had planned our itinerary very carefully to provide the best opportunity for success.

From this location, we traveled a short distance inland to A.D. Barnes Park, where, except for an eccentric gentleman famous for feeding the feral cats in this and other Miami-area parks, we were the only people present. Neither the cat lover nor the well-fed cats appeared to pose a threat. We waited to hear the call of a LaSagra's Flycatcher, often necessary to locate this bird, which is native to the Bahamas but is a regular stray to South Florida. We heard the call, but a Cooper's Hawk appeared and spooked the flycatcher, which became silent and could not be located. The hawk fortunately departed, but it was another 30 minutes or so before we heard the flycatcher utter its high-pitched "wink!" It had moved to a different location at the far edge of the park.

This time, we were able to locate the bird, and I was able to see all his field marks. The yellow breast can be seen only in direct light; otherwise, it looks white and unmarked. The head is relatively large and crested, although the crest is not always visible.

The wings have inconspicuous white wing bars. There is almost no rufous in the tail, which distinguishes it from other Myiarchus flycatchers native to the United States. The head, back, and tail are dark brown to black. Its call is a distinctive single note, high-pitched and descending. This coveted bird could be missed easily,

LaSagra's Flycatcher

Cooper's Hawk
Photograph by Noam Dahary

especially if there is any noise. That is why finding it early in the day before the arrival of the revelers is optimum and was part of Larry's well-conceived plan.

After another short drive, we arrived at Bill Baggs Park, which had a paved path through some trees bearing spring fruit, the preferred habitat for the Thick-billed Vireo. Other birders had seen it already, and after a short wait, it appeared and displayed itself shamelessly and without hesitation, close enough to make it difficult and unnecessary to focus my binocs. This vireo is a small songbird with a substantial bill appropriate for catching live prey. I noted its mostly green and yellow belly, the characteristic yellow lores in front of its eyes, and a partial light eye ring.

Lores: The part of the face in front of the eyes that may give the impression of spectacles. Birds don't commonly wear these since their eyes are on the sides of their heads, except for owls which wisely refuse to wear them.

We heard its song too, best described as scolding or gossipy, very similar to that of the White-eyed Vireo, which is common in this habitat. It is truly a rare bird, the only one seen that year. This vireo, like the La Sagra's Flycatcher, nests in the Bahamas but strays to South Florida unpredictably, perhaps to play a little shuffleboard.

Thanks to Larry's itinerary and prowess I had seen three life birds before 10 a.m.

Thick-billed Vireo
Photograph Provided by Larry Manfredi

White-eyed Parakeet
Photograph by Larry Manfredi

Joe's Stone Crab was only about a mile from my Art Deco hotel in Miami Beach, and we agreed to meet for dinner there again as we had on my previous trip, establishing a small tradition. Rituals can enrich life if chosen carefully, and this had become one of those. I checked into my hotel, a modernized iteration of the historic Palmer House Hotel, and fell into a coma from which I awoke a couple of hours later, much improved and ready for dinner.

I arrived at Joe's ahead of Larry at about 5:30, put our names on the list, and found a seat at the venerable bar, which was tended by a handsome, aging bartender who had been there for many years. On a whim, I asked him if he remembered the name Arenson and told him about my late great-aunt, great-uncle, and parents, who had been there frequently over the last several decades. I was amazed and pleased to hear him say that he did recall the name and perhaps the people as well. He asked some questions which suggested his memory was accurate. He recalled that my father was a boat builder (he did build one in Toledo where I grew up), and he also gave a credible description of my uncle, a tiny man with a full head of white hair in his nineties. He told me that he had been the bartender there for 37 years—all these things fit.

I became even more nostalgic than I usually do when I go to Joe's. I mentioned that I was nearly 74 years old. This surprised him, which pleased (or at least flattered) me, and he produced a great vodka martini. We reminisced as I sipped the strong drink on an empty stomach.

Bronzed Cowbird
Photograph by Larry Manfredi

Brown-headed Cowbird
Photograph by Larry Manfredi

The next morning Larry picked me up at a diner adjacent to the hotel. As we exited the café, we heard a cacophony of squawks and found a flock of White-eyed Parakeets in one of the few trees left on this old street in old Miami Beach.

Before the day ended, we would find two other species of parakeets, the Green and the Red-masked. We had lunch and drove to Homestead, Florida, the gateway to the Everglades, where we planned to sit in the shade in Larry's backyard and look for the three species of cowbirds and the Painted Buntings that live there. We got good looks at all these birds. I don't know any other place in North America where all three species of cowbirds can be seen. This is something that only a devout birder could love. We were joined in this enterprise by Larry's old Doberman, Shadow, who immediately attached herself to me, the dog magnet.

I hadn't seen Shiny or Bronzed Cowbirds or Painted Buntings for many years, and it was especially interesting to compare the three cowbirds. They get their names from the propensity to be, whenever possible, near or riding on cows, which scare up insects for them to devour. The Brown-headed Cowbird, discussed in my chapter on Kirtland's Warbler, was partly responsible for the warbler's alarming decline. Many Brown-headed Cowbirds perished to save the rare warbler, but not in vain—the program was successful.

Finally, Larry and I wrestled ourselves out of our chairs and headed for the airport area to look for more exotics. We found two of these, Green Parakeets and Red-crowned Parrots, after driving erratically around an urban neighborhood between the airport and

Shiny Cowbird
Photograph by Larry Manfredi

Painted Bunting
Photograph by Larry Manfredi

Hialeah racetrack, two treeless areas. We landed at a local watering hole called Woody's West End Tavern, where we found the nesting Red-crowned Parrots. Woody's has the dubious distinction of being frequented by local birding guides and their clients, one of whom was a friend of Larry's who apparently lost his marriage as a result of his shenanigans at the Tavern.

We got into comparatively less trouble there, and afterwards Larry dropped me off at the airport for the flight home. This had been a wondrous trip, as was the previous one, with a truly special person whose skills as a nature guide, including knowledge of plants, trees, butterflies, and anything else that is alive, are as extraordinary as his endearing eccentricities. We parted company with the hope that we would be on another adventure soon in Florida or the Bahamas or some other bird-and birder-infested destination.

Of course, there's always a balance of success, failure, and irony in these escapades. This one was no exception. After I arrived safely home in Denver, I read in the newspaper that the Boeing 737 Mack 8, the aircraft on which I flew home, had been grounded in most other countries—but inexplicably not in the United States—due to a series of fatal crashes. I also noted the day after my return that the Bananaquit, which had been missing for many days, was seen again at a park where we were unable to locate it.

Less than a year later, Larry's advice was once again indispensable in searching for another life bird. My wife Aura and I were in Florida and, having traveled on a commuter boat from Fort Myers to Key West, we were planning to pursue Antillean Nighthawks

Green Parakeets - Photograph by Larry Manfredi

at the airport on Marathon Key. I called Larry for his advice, which helped us find the bird in time to get back to Key West and eat a whole roasted red snapper. ("Not a fillet!")

The meal likely saved our marriage, and although it took about 25 years to find, I now had another bird I had missed years before on my trip to the Dry Tortugas. My list was now north of 750, about 10 times my age and still growing—even if I had begun to shrink like the Baird's sparrow population in North Dakota.

RULE 15
Any creative behavior is likely to be met with suspicion,
especially if it involves crossing borders or your
neighbor's driveway.

About 2002, I decided to make a late spring trip to North Dakota in search of the nesting (and singing) Baird's Sparrow, Sprague's Pipit, and other coveted birds. I found two guys (let's call them Sven and Ole) offering personal guide service, and I signed up.

I had never been to North Dakota and imagined it to be a flat wasteland with lots of grass and a few bovine farmers. I decided to save money and avoid the puddle-jumper from Minneapolis by flying directly from Denver to Winnipeg, Manitoba, then driving across the border into North Dakota, where I would meet my pair of guides. I would save a little on the trip's CPB (cost per bird), and I would even get to see a little of Canada.

I couldn't have imagined, even in a nightmare, that years later I would be near Winnipeg heading the other direction, racing to cross from the United States into Canada at a border crossing called Pembina. We were on our way to our seasonal residence in Cape Breton to escape the COVID pandemic, along with the first Trump administration's poor management of the crisis.

I got off the plane and told the Border Control Officer my plans. He looked at me in disbelief and moved me and my luggage to a separate room where everything was ransacked and inspected. I felt like Arlo Guthrie in Alice's Restaurant when the real criminals moved to another bench after they heard that he was charged with littering. The fact that I had field guides, binoculars, and a scope did not seem to be enough. An hour later, with a blood pressure of about 500 mmHg, I was finally cleared, got my car, and called my guides to let them know I would be late.

Grey Partridge

Baird's Sparrow

Sven and Ole were jolly when they met me on the US side of the border and took me to a nice cabin by a lake to get some rest and be ready to head out (yep) early in the morning. I hadn't expected much from North Dakota, other than the birds, but I was pleasantly surprised. The prairie, when not replaced by farms, is pristine with its rolling terrain with countless scattered lakes created by glaciers during the last Ice Age. I awoke in our cabin to a cacophony of singing birds and breeding Red-necked Grebes on the lake.

We started our day at dawn and drove along unpaved country roads in search of Grey Partridges, finding them quite easily. The secret is to be early, and we were. On the way, I had already heard the first of a litany of "Sven and Ole" jokes. Most of these are unfit for a book like this, but here's one example: Sven and Ole took a trip to the beach where they hoped to find female companionship. While Sven had no problem in this enterprise, Ole became frustrated and asked Sven for advice. Sven suggested walking up and down the beach with a potato in his Speedo. Ole did this and returned to tell Sven that his stroll down the beach was met with jeers and laughter. Sven admonished Ole, "I thought I told you to put da podado in front!"

Next on the agenda was Sprague's Pipit. This bird prefers the prairie and has the notable behavior of flying very high during breeding and singing from the sky with an enchanting song. Once the song is heard, it is possible to locate the bird above and observe its characteristic flight pattern. A chiropractor would be handy afterward. By this time, I was beginning to realize how beautiful this land was, at least at that time of year, late spring, when the temperature was perfect. It is a land of open prairie, with glacial lakes surrounded by hills and trees, all redolent with wildlife and especially birds.

The most important target bird for this trip was Baird's Sparrow, which is in serious decline. We would have to do "a bit" of driving—about two hours. These sparrows are thinly distributed and rare, even in their prime territory. It took us several more hours to locate a singing Baird's Sparrow, which was perched on a twiggy bush. We could see its pale white breast decorated with a necklace of dark brown streaks. The song consists of a couple of sharp notes, followed by a long, high-pitched trill. The echo almost seems to overlap the next cycle, which occurs every six seconds. It is my opinion that this is one of the most compelling and memorable songs of any bird.

Song: That which may be heard when a bird sings if it is a bird that can sing and chooses to do so.

I was thrilled, but at the same time, concerned about the bird's precarious status. Accordingly, I wrote this poem:

Last Song

in shrinking tall grass prairie
a sparrow, Baird's
never common now scarce
perches on a thistle stalk

necklaced on its creamy breast
displayed to lure a mate to nest
calls out in notes so delicate
a breath of wind disguises it

a song that rings like tinny bells
windblown chimes from distant hills
waits for the acknowledgment
heard each spring since
god knows when

those chirpy acquiescences
the promise of a brood well-bred
the promise of a legacy

but soon I fear
a spring will come
when all he hears is….

Having spotted our Baird's, we then searched high and low and everywhere in between for Nelson's Sparrow. This bird had been split from the Sharp-tailed Sparrow I'd seen years ago on the coast of Georgia into Saltmarsh and Nelson's Sparrows. The latter breeds from North Dakota north into Canada, and also in coastal Nova Scotia and Quebec. Its "song" is very brief and strange, comparable to the sound of sizzling bacon. After miles of walking, we heard the call but were never able to see this bird, which likes to skulk in wet grass or marsh. (I eventually got a brief look at one in coastal Texas in winter, but it was silent. I finally got both the call and the bird in Cape Breton at Point Michaud many years later.)

I still get a special feeling of peacefulness when I think of North Dakota, where the town of Minot is best known for the question, "Why not Minot?" and the answer, "Freezin's the reason." Go in spring—the birds know what they're doing—and don't worry about Fargo; just don't go there or, if you do, stay away from murderous used car salesmen with woodchippers.

Just one more anecdote from my dynamic guides. Sven and Ole got married in a double ceremony to Lena and Helga, respectively. They agreed to keep track of their wedding night pleasures by making vertical marks on the bedsteads with their Swiss army knives. Sven made two lines and Ole, three. When Sven saw Ole's bed he exclaimed, "By golly, you got me der, Ole. I got two, but 111 musta kept you up all night, yah?"

Yellow Rail

Spruce Grouse

THE YELLOW RAILS OF
MCGREGOR MARSH, MINNESOTA

RULE 16
In birding, as in everything else, family comes first,
for the birder and the birds.

Minnesota, a state well known for its friendly and well-educated people, as well as its impressive list of hard-to-find birds, is one of the best places to find a small, unaccommodating, mostly nocturnal bird called the Yellow Rail. This rail, like most other rails, lives in inhospitable, swampy areas where a birder can be eaten alive by mosquitoes while sinking precariously into mud as sticky as molasses—and still not catch a glimpse of this frustrating bird. McGregor Marsh, in northern Minnesota near the town of Brainerd, is a place where some have been fortunate enough to see it, usually lucky just to get a brief glimpse in a flashlight beam after calling a male out of the gloom by playing a tape or tapping pebbles together to mimic its call. The males come toward the sound to defend their territory from other lonely males, but flit away quickly to defend their romance.

I had been birding in Minnesota before, as part of a trip to run the famous Grandma's Marathon, which ends in Duluth after following along the north shore of Lake Superior, called *Kitchi-Gami* in Chippewa and Ojibway. I had seen my only LeConte's Sparrow as well as my first Mourning Warbler. I also found a Spruce Grouse near Ely, where I canoed as a teenager during summer camp.

In 2002, I persuaded my teenage, not-quite-birder daughter, Patty, to accompany me on an organized weekend trip to northern Minnesota in spring to see many coveted species, including the coveted Yellow Rail. Patty got to spend a few days with a friend in Minneapolis, then we departed for the north.

The tour was full, but its benevolent guide, Kim Eckert, author of *A Birder's Guide to Minnesota*, was generous enough to let us tag along. We stayed in Brainerd, where we heard the musical Minnesota accent spoken by our cheerful and loquacious receptionist. I found it endearing since I grew up in Ohio, where the speech was similar but less exuberant. Some examples are leaving the "g" out of "ing" (smokin' or cookin'), and Scandinavian expressions such as "you bet ya, eh!" and "Oh yaaaaaaah." The addition of an extra syllable to words like goat (go-at) and toast (to-ast) is often heard.

The Minnesotans themselves are a likeable lot, but one word of caution for visiting birders: Minnesota woodlands harbor some of the world's most aggressive mosquitos and Black-legged ticks, which carry Lyme disease and several others. Precautions must be taken to avoid these critters. Yes, they are God's creations, but I'm confident that my disdain for them will be forgiven.

We checked in, rushed to get some fast food, and joined the group before dusk at McGregor Marsh, which appeared impenetrable. Our only chance was to induce the diminutive Yellow Rail to come to us. Before the calling began, we were treated to skyrocketing winnowing Wilson's Snipes and the ventriloquistic call—rattle might be a better word—of Nelson's Sharp-tailed Sparrow, which we were unable to see (again) even though they were only feet away. Once it got dark, we focused on a clearing that extended into the marsh where Kim placed a tape recorder, turned on a repeating tape of the rail, and instructed us to sit still, listen, and wait — all of which are challenges for birders. The bird was calling from a considerable distance out in the impregnable swamp.

We held our breath and listened silently as the bird approached the clearing in response to the provocative sounds

Connecticut Warbler

Palette Abstract of Yellow Rail
and Connecticut Warbler

from the tape recorder. Eventually, the movement stopped, but not the calling, and we were instructed to switch on our lights and aim toward the sound. The sudden burst of light revealed our bird standing befuddled on the machine, apparently confused, if not angry at these intruders who certainly were not a threat and bore no resemblance to a competing rail. The hoodwinked bird promptly thumbed its version of the proverbial middle finger at us and vanished. Even my less-than-enthusiastic daughter was thrilled by this outcome, and after a few subdued high-fives, we retired with instructions to meet at daybreak for the next day's outing. In this case, the early departure took its toll on my daughter and me.

We awoke on time the next morning with throaty protests from my daughter, who is not a morning person (thus, not a birder), met the group, and headed north to the Sax-Zim Bog, northwest of Duluth. The Bog is famous as a place to see the Connecticut Warbler, Yellow-bellied Flycatcher, Boreal Chickadee, Sharp-tailed Grouse, and Great Grey Owl, among others. Of course, our trusty guide had thoroughly scouted the area in advance to optimize our chances. We found all these birds except the Boreal Chickadee, which I had already seen in Maine and would later have in my yard in Cape Breton, Nova Scotia. The Connecticut Warbler was a great thrill for me and another lifer. It is very elusive, even for a warbler, even when you find it where it sings and breeds. This warbler sings with passion and defends its territory, but seldom reveals itself.

My daughter, however, was so exhausted that she insisted on sleeping in the car, and we needed to make the long drive back to

Minneapolis that day. Thus, I decided to concede to my daughter's torpor and forgo seeing the Great Grey Owl that I had seen once but only briefly in Yosemite National Park.

 *I didn't realize it at the time, but I was beginning to bear some resemblance to this grey raptor.*

These are the common conflicts that arise when birders have other responsibilities. I believe my daughter appreciated my paternal decision (probably too lenient), and she will never forget the Yellow Rail experience—even if she is unlikely to ever see the magnificent Great Grey Owl. My painting of the Yellow Rail now hangs in her apartment.

WAR, LOSS, AND SURVIVAL:
CERULEAN WARBLERS IN VIRGINIA

Just a few years ago, about 2015, I made a trip east in spring to visit my dear friend and biking companion from Colorado, Nancy Powers, PhD., who was at Sloan-Kettering Cancer Center in New York with an incurable, rare abdominal cancer that kept her from digesting anything. She suffered greatly and survived only a few months after my visit. Even though oncology is my field, I have never been able to accept the great suffering that innocent people must endure, and this was a prime example.

I had a good visit with Nancy and a wonderful meal at Le Perigord, my favorite New York neighborhood restaurant.

It was there that I once observed a well-dressed solitary gentleman, aged about 80 years, drink a bottle of vintage Bordeaux while reading Hamlet from beginning to end—only in New York.

Of course, I felt guilty about enjoying the food so much, knowing that Nancy was starving and couldn't eat a thing. I offered to bring her anything she wanted, but she declined. I recall eating sweetbreads and *foie gras* served by a seasoned server in a black tuxedo. Sadly, the COVID pandemic ended this illustrious eatery.

I decided to use the opportunity of being in the east in spring to look for the declining Cerulean Warbler, which I had never seen. I wanted to hear it sing, as it only does briefly in spring, and see it low in the leafless trees before it established its typical territory high in the forest canopy. I had done my homework and found that Virginia, near the nation's capital, was the best spot. I even found a pair of young biologists willing to show me around; they knew within a narrow window when the birds would arrive from their wintering grounds in Mexico and Central America.

We set out at dawn and arrived in a national forest where several varieties of trillium were blooming everywhere. My hosts were a little anxious because we were so close to the birds' expected arrival. However, it didn't take long to hear the song and spot the birds. The foliage was sparse enough and the birds were low enough that I got great looks, seldom the case with many species of warbler. I had prepared well, one of the most important determinants of successful birding, by getting advice about Cerulean Warblers from another Colorado birder who was much more experienced than I.

The plumage of these birds was primarily a soft blue (hence the name cerulean) with handsome but delicate black striping on their flanks. In the correct light, the blue on their cap was iridescent. They had two white wing bars and a blue band across the throat. The song was an initial series of notes introducing another series of ascending ones, quite distinct and frequent. I am blessed with good high-pitch hearing (my sight is not nearly as good), but for those who cannot hear high frequencies, this song might not be heard.

My informal research with patients revealed that high-frequency hearing loss predominantly occurs on the side where the spouse sleeps.

In this case, because they had not yet produced young, we did not see their unusual behavior known as "bungeeing," in which, to protect their fledglings by distracting predators, they plunge several feet from the nest before coming out of their dive and finding a perch.

Cerulean Warblers are classified as "vulnerable" and have decreased 26% each decade since the early 20th century—an overall decrease of 70%. Habitat loss seems to be the main issue, and there is little prospect of stopping the decline, although projects have been initiated to preserve critical areas by cutting clearings in old forests. This bird prefers old-growth forests with mixed hardwood and pine and, as I already indicated, prefers to be high in the canopy. It was a great joy to see these jewels so well with such knowledgeable hosts who also showed me some rare varieties of orchid, the Lady's Slipper, that they had scouted in advance for me.

It was a very humid spring day compared to what I am used to in Colorado. I sweated through my leather watchband and later had to replace it. As we drove through the rolling hills of the Virginia

Cerulean Warbler - Seen near
Antietam Battlefield in Virginia

The Road to Antietam

Piedmont, I began recognizing names of places where much of the Civil War played out, names like Harper's Ferry and Antietam. On September 17, 1862, the latter was the site of one of the bloodiest battles of the war. Although neither side could claim victory from the Battle of Antietam (also known as Sharpsburg), the conflict ended the northward thrust of the Confederacy, which previously had gone unfettered. There were 22,717 casualties. Now, the site is a green, pristine park in which only a few markers reveal the needless carnage that took place there. This battleground, the warbler, and Nancy's tragic illness converged in a poem which I wrote on my flight home:

Cerulean Blue

Virginia forest
early spring
just arrived
from winter haunts
ascending trills
descend from perches
high above in primal trees

enlarged to brilliance
in my glass
its marks precise
in muted blue
cerulean warbler
a dwindling jewel
seen just in time

just miles away
as warblers fly
a battleground
Antietam Antietam
the warblers chant
bloodiest of that bloody War

observed by their progeny
are fertilized fields
of fallen soldiers
orchids and trillium
rare like the warblers
but safe for the moment
their battle, like Antietam
still not won

If you watch "The Battle of Antietam" in Ken Burns's brilliant Civil War documentary, listen for the Cerulean Warblers singing in the background, descendants of those who observed the battle.

Green Jay

Brown Jay

THE RIO GRANDE VALLEY OF TEXAS

RULE 18
When all is dark, listen.

My first visit to the Rio Grande Valley of Texas took place soon after I returned to Denver in 1988, where I would finish the last 32 years of my medical career. I had dreamed of going to the Valley and had read extensively about its avifauna. I finally decided to go solo to take it all in. I knew I would need many trips to see the specialty birds that are spread over many miles in various habitats.

The Rio Grande Valley occupies the triangular southern tip of Texas, where the Rio Grande River, the headwaters of which are in the Colorado Rockies, makes its final descent to the Gulf of Mexico at Brownsville. It is a warm, damp, semi-tropical region with areas of lush flora that provide a variety of habitats for wildlife, especially birds. Lying along the Mexican border from Big Bend National Park to the Gulf, it is inhabited by a variety of birds that are more typical of Mexico and includes strays from Central and South America. One of the issues, well known only to frustrated birders, is that there are times when a bird is spotted only on the Mexican side of the border, and thus cannot be counted on an American Birding Association life list. The best example of this is the enormous and raucous Brown Jay. Birders would wait for hours trying to induce the stubborn birds to cross the river, often to no avail.

Between Falcon Dam, which is itself an excellent spot for certain species, and the Gulf of Mexico are a series of well-known locations and refuges where most of the sought-after birds are found. These include Salineño, a nondescript spot on the river, Santa Margarita Ranch, Bentsen State Park, Santa Ana Refuge, Estero Llano Park, Weslaco, Hidalgo, and Sable Palms Refuge. Along the coast, heading toward Corpus Christi, are several more areas, including Aransas, where the Whooping Cranes winter, and the famous Big Thicket, which is a concentration point for migrants. More recently, the campus of the University of Texas Rio Grande Valley, (UTRGV) has become another hot spot, as we shall see.

I flew in the evening to Laredo where I spent the night in a marginal motel with a few six-legged "visitors" scratching around all night. I awoke early, found breakfast, and headed down the Valley. As I drove, many birds I had never or seldom seen—such as Scissor-tailed Flycatchers and Crested Caracaras—already dotted my route. Many species of raptors I hadn't seen were also present, including Harris's Hawk.

I visited several of the refuges, where I easily found many of the specialty birds that are often colorful or noisy enough to be conspicuous. At that time, Bentsen State Park allowed "snowbirds" to park their caravans on its grounds, where many fed the birds with feeders and fruit. Although a campground full of RVs might not be the most romantic place to find birds, it was productive, and the visitors, for the most part, were jovial and friendly to the birders. This is how I found my first Clay-colored Thrush and enjoyed many Altamira Orioles eating oranges impaled on sticks. There was a telephone pole in Bentsen in which nested a tiny Elf Owl. The owl emerged predictably from its hole at about 7 p.m. each night to a crowd of dozens of birders.

On this first trip to Texas, I made it to the Aransas National Wildlife Refuge on the Gulf Coast, where I was able to take a guided boat ride to see Whooping Cranes. These unique birds were and still are endangered, but have been saved by captive breeding, like the California Condors. Thus, I added the crane to my list of some of the most endangered birds in North America. I knew already that I would return to this birdy area many times.

By the late nineties, I had made several unsuccessful and frustrating attempts to see Hook-billed Kites. These raptors exclusively eat snails, so they appear only in years with enough rain to support the tasty mollusks. The best way to see them is to walk early in the

Elf Owl

Ferruginous Pygmy Owl

morning, before the tram is running, about a mile to an observation deck in Bentsen State Park. From the deck, the kite can be seen fl ying to its feeding grounds—if you are very lucky.

I never was, and the deck, while a good place to see other birds, is hot and unsheltered with no *agua* or *baño*. My trusty guide of several trips, Darrell, was just as frustrated as I was. We never seemed to be in the right place at the right time. We got back to the parking lot to race to the airport for my fl ight home and were forced to listen to a couple brag loudly enough that they could be heard in Dallas about the great looks they had just gotten of a Hook-billed Kite roosting in a tree.

This is the taunting behavior of a minority of birders who give the rest a bad rap. The kite had become a "nemesis bird."

One of my visits was with Travis Wilkins, a guide who lived on a ranch west of Houston with his wife, Anelle. He collected me at the airport and drove me to his ranch, where we spent the night before setting out early the next day. We found an area populated by thousands of migrating shorebirds, among which we found a few Buff-breasted Sandpipers—my first look at this bird. We also found Groove-billed Anis and Audubon's Orioles in the Valley.

Perhaps the best was saved for last. When we returned to his ranch, Travis took me to a tree where there was a nest of White-

Masked Duck

tailed Hawks, again my first. (He also found a huge rattlesnake on the road. To my astonishment, he managed to catch it with a hooked stick, which he waved at me, belly-laughing, before releasing the agitated serpent.)

Still, despite the long list of desirable birds that I managed to see in the Valley over the years, including the Ferruginous Pygmy Owl and Masked Duck, there remained a few painful misses. One year, I arrived one day too late to see a Bare-throated Tiger Heron that had been easily seen daily at the Santa Ana Refuge. The same thing happened with a Roadside Hawk. Another time, a Blue Bunting flew into view at Estero Llano Grande Park, but I couldn't get my glasses on it, much to the dismay of my guide.

And on top of it all, there were several failed attempts to find a Hook-billed Kite.

Finally, a good story about Bentsen State Park.

The refuge was named after the former Senator Lloyd Bentsen, when there were still Democrats elected to office in Texas.

Darrell and I decided to do some night birding in the Refuge. We walked in the twilight, having forgotten to bring flashlights, but there was enough light to see some of the night birds. We saw Common Pauraques, which are similar to Whip-poor-wills, and many Eastern Screech Owls, which were constantly calling. The Common Chachalacas, a large and loud fowl, were squawking. Many dragonflies and moths filled the warm, humid air. The night had its unique pungent smells, including the contributions of the malodorous and musky resident javelinas. Fog closed in. As we walked, a pair of huge black tarantulas crossed our path, oblivious to our presence. We were alone in this wild, dark, and unfamiliar place. Then, fortuitously, we heard accordion music from somewhere across the river in Mexico and some joyful singing in Spanish. This provided comfort to us in the mysterious gloom. We felt a kinship with our unseen compadres, and I wrote this poem:

Night Music

a moonless night
in the Rio Grande Valley

Pauraques squawk
in mesquite tangles
darting for spiders and bugs

screech owls moan
like fading lives
in hospital halls

we walk in darkness
flashlights carelessly
left behind

pause while
tarantulas
cross our path

humidity descends
a long lonely walk
intruders in the wild

across the river in Mexico
unseen compadres
brighten our night

an accordion sings
a Mexican waltz

And so it went, as is so often the case, the good with the bad, isolation and darkness enlightened by the musical comfort of unseen amigos from another world.

.

RULE 19
Our upright posture separates us from the apes,
so for Darwin's sake, stand up and walk.

One of the best day hikes of my life was in the cool, dry, 5 a.m. Texas air of the Chisos Mountains of Big Bend National Park with guide Darrell Vollert and photographer Dr. David McDonald in 1997. We were in search of the Colima Warbler. David was schlepping an enormous lens and camera along with his water, food, and self. I offered to help, but the offer was declined, probably because he didn't trust me not to drop his very pricey gear. Or maybe he simply wanted the exercise. I respected his decision, and he managed to schlepp the aforementioned goods a full 12 miles until we returned to our quarters.

Schlepp: An onomatopoetic Yiddish word for moving something from one place to another with suffering.

I cannot recall the altitude we reached before we heard our first Colima, but I do remember that it was as we had predicted. This warbler breeds from 3,000 to 9,000 feet but can adapt, if necessary, to lower elevations. Its song is distinctive and loud and consists of a trill completed by three or four ascending and descending emphatic notes. That morning, we saw and heard them in full song. We decided to count our steps between singing warblers as we continued along the trail. We were surprised by how close the singing males were to each other—about 30 to 40 paces. We heard and saw many until we had descended to a point on the trail where they suddenly disappeared. I was so overwhelmed with this bird that I don't recall anything else we saw on this very long hike. We could have doubled back and saved our legs, but we were adventurous and continued for the full 12 miles. It was a long and memorable day. The contrast between the lush montane vegetation and the dry rocky terrain below stands out in my memory.

Lucifer Hummingbird
Photograph Provided by
Dr. David McDonald

Satellite View of Big Bend National Park
Painted by Author and Shown with
Permission of Judy Lane, MD, Owner

The only place to see Colima Warbler in North American is Big Bend National Park in West Texas. The park is relatively lightly used since it is so remote. We flew into El Paso and drove from there. The geography is spectacular, as are the plants, some of which are found nowhere else. So, of course, are the birds.

Our first stop was the Davis Mountains, where we sat at a site reputed to be the most reliable place in North America to see and photograph Montezuma Quail, which had become one of my nemesis birds. They come to the site regularly to get water from a continuously dripping fountain (similar to the dripping fountain on Garden Key) where there is a shady place to sit and wait, wait and sit, and that is what we did. We never saw the quail. But we had great birding, including several species of flycatchers, as is often the case when you are in the right place and stay there instead of wandering around to less productive places. Later, after we gave up on quail, we spooked and flushed one on a hike into the Davis Mountains, but got a poor look. There we saw many Grace's Warblers and other southern warblers. We also had great looks at Zone-tailed Hawks.

We eventually left this area and headed for Big Bend, stopping along the way in a small West Texas town for a West Texas meal and some West Texas beer, where we shared some West Texas lies and joked about West Texas. David and Darrell were the Texans; I, the token Yankee.

The drive into Big Bend is long and very beautiful—if you can appreciate the beauty of nothingness, which I do. We checked into our adequate rooms, ate, and hit the hay to rise at dawn for the long and steep trek into Boot Spring in the Chisos Hills, in quest for the Colima Warbler. This hike is legendary among birders, some of whom have hired donkeys or horses to avoid the walk. We were able to make it on foot, which I believe is the best way if you can do it.

The park rangers had warned us about dehydration, and we were well prepared. They have to rescue people every day who are not well prepared or don't listen, whether they've been warned about water, trail safety, or anything else. For example, there is an enticing trail that descends steeply from the parking lot of the main lodge. What goes up must come down, but the opposite is not necessarily true: Each day, the rangers must go down this trail to rescue visitors who go down but can't manage the climb back.

As a physician who has seen firsthand the all-around benefits of an active lifestyle, I feel compelled at this juncture to climb onto my soapbox about physical fitness. (Don't worry—I'll be able to get down again.)

Since we no longer have to chase our food to avoid starvation, although we still have the genes to do so, we simply must choose to exercise. This is a choice infrequently made these days, except by young people in urban environments, which are littered with places to exercise and offer a strange buffet of niche options. I even once heard about a "goat yoga" studio, in which the yoga is conducted in the presence of loose goats, which do what goats do as the yoga practitioners do what they do. I am hoping to give this a try.

I had a plan a few years ago that involved goats. I lived in a suburb of Denver blessed with an owner's association that was empowered to send spies around the neighborhood trolling for egregious infractions of the association's rules, which included "harboring barnyard animals." (I guess this rule was meant to discourage people who could afford expensive houses, but still wanted to own cows, chickens, pigs, or—God forbid—goats.)

I planned to purchase one or two pygmy goats and let them loose in the open space behind my house, where they would keep the weeds under control and, in the process, protect the property from wildfires. I would house them in a pen at night. I anticipated that within a few days at most, I would be cited for "harboring barnyard

Colima Warbler - Photograph Provided by Dr. David McDonald

animals," and my rehearsed response would be that these were a rare breed of dog that only resembled—but were not—goats. I would demand that they prove these were goats and not dogs. DNA testing would be required, which I would likely be forced to pay for alongside a hefty fine when the jig was finally up.

I still regret not doing this, but my wife, Julie, persuaded me to desist. We are now divorced, and she still lives in the same place, whilst I have escaped.

But I digress; we need to change our attitude about exercise and get healthier. The cost of healthcare, speaking as a physician who was still in practice nearly 50 years after medical school, is enormous and growing exponentially. Much of this is attributable to lifestyle issues, the excessive intake of carbohydrates and animal fat, and the lack of exercise. These behaviors could change if they were taken as seriously as they should be. I don't want to be un-American, even

Varied Bunting
Photograph provided by Dr. David McDonald

Varied Bunting
Painting by Aura Arenson

though I have moved to Canada. However, Coke, Pepsi, fossil fuel, and yes, bovine farts have done more damage than cigarettes and certainly more than goats. End of rant.

After our magnificent trek to see the Colima Warbler, we rested, ate something, and headed out for some evening birding. We saw some good birds, including singing Black-chinned Sparrows, by walking down the aforementioned trail famous for numerous daily rescues. Notably, we were able to walk up the same trail. Later, we found two more life birds—a Common Black Hawk on its nest along the Rio Grande River and a Lucifer Hummingbird. Despite these good things, the trip is best remembered for the Colima Warblers, the hike to find them, and the West Texas camaraderie.

Finally, David managed to get a great photo of a perched male Varied Bunting. This photograph so inspired me that I made a painting of it, as did my wife, Aura. Her painting shows great appreciation for the striking colors and details of this bird, even though she wisely denies being a birder, which has preserved her excellent reputation. The life birds I found on this adventure are sine qua non for lifers who are trying to achieve an impressive life list. I was on my way and closer than I thought.

NEWFOUNDLAND IN SPRING

I first visited Newfoundland in search of a Northern Lapwing, a European bird that is a rarity in winter in Atlantic Canada. The details of this misadventure are presented in a subsequent episode in which the bird, which we missed in Newfoundland, was finally seen in Nova Scotia.

However, we decided to return to Newfoundland in the spring of 2011, hoping to see icebergs (not Jewish) and to find a European Golden Plover, a bird that often appears briefly in low numbers. We were counseled that a perfect spot to do these things was a town called Bona Vista, at the eastern tip of the next peninsula north of St. John's, the provincial capital. Bona Vista is about a three-hour drive from St. John's. From its coastline of lyrical beauty, which is virtually uninhabited, you can walk for hours and never see another person as you gaze toward the site of the sinking of the *Titanic* on April 15, 1912, about 200 kilometers to the east.

Bona Vista is a fishing village, and in the spring, lobster season begins and snow crab season is in full bloom. The elegant lady who rented us two lovely cottages with a spectacular view arranged for enormous lobsters to be delivered to us straight from the traps on opening day at a very reasonable price.

For this trip, we persuaded our recently married friends, Glen and Alice, to join us. Glen was an amateur but very skillful photographer, and Alice was a pathologist, a concert-level classical musician, and an adventurer open to practically anything. Alice and I had become friends during her days as a pathologist. She attended our weekly brain tumor conference and eloquently described the microscopic findings of the tumor biopsies. She moved away to New York to resume her musical passion and fell in love with Glen. Aura and I attended their wedding in an empty building along the Hudson. We danced a tango on one of the piers. Now, we had asked them to join us in Newfoundland and were surprised and overjoyed that they decided to be part of our adventure.

Atlantic Puffin - Photograph provided
by Glen Myers

An Explosion of Seabirds
Painting by Edward Arenson after
photograph by Glen Myers

We met in St. John's, where we all arrived, this time, without calamity or weather issues. We had dinner together to catch up and set out for some carousing on George Street. We found a pub with good Celtic music that included a fiddler. Alice expressed an interest in sitting in for a song or two, so I went up to the stage and asked if she could. The musician seemed a bit skeptical until I explained that Alice was a Juilliard-trained violinist. He invited her to the stage, where she performed admirably while Aura and I danced a Celtic waltz.

The next day we traveled to the coast, where we took a boat to a seabird island in the Witless Bay Ecological Reserve, which hosts thousands, perhaps millions, of nesting Murres, both Common and Thick-billed, Razor-billed Auks, Atlantic Puffins, Fulmars, and Black-legged Kittiwakes. The rock is a rich rose color, decorated with millennia of guano and moss. Glen took innumerable photographs, which led to a few of my better paintings, some of which are shown here.

As the boat traversed the calm waters around the island, thousands of Murres rose from the sea in the path of the boat and produced clouds of sea foam, all of which recalled the abstract paintings of Jackson Pollock and led to the painting shown. A Bald Eagle hovered over the nesting birds and created quite a disturbance but took no prey. It was a glorious day of sights, sounds, and smells preserved by Glen's camera. I started thinking about learning photography.

The next day, we traveled to Bona Vista and checked into our beautifully appointed cottages. We explored the postcard fishing

Black-Legged Kittiwakes of Witless Bay
Photograph Provided by Glen Myers

Black-Footed Kittiwakes of Witless
Bay Painting by Edward Arenson
After Photograph by Glen Myers

village and found the docks where the crabs were stored. We asked the fishermen for a few and were shown some that were rejected by Alice, who indicated that she was Korean, and therefore not going to be fooled. We wound up with much larger specimens at a reasonable price and returned to our cozy shelters. Our spouses remained in the car, uninterested in the snow crabs.

Both Aura and Glen keep kosher, a litany of biblical dietary restrictions by which some Jews punish themselves for being the "Chosen People". The Jewish dietary laws are a major point of contention between orthodox Jews and various more modern iterations who enjoy food.

We found some fresh salmon for them instead, and they were happy.

The next morning, our lobsters were delivered. Since Alice and I could not eat all or even most of the crab and lobster, we mixed the leftovers, and I cooked seafood omelets the following morning while our spouses religiously ate their cereal. I would have been more sympathetic, but I knew they didn't know what they were missing. Since there was still leftover seafood, we made mayonnaise and had lobster and crab rolls for lunch.

Early the next morning, I ventured forth to an open grassy area on the ridge that runs to the headland called Point Bona Vista and trudged around randomly with my binoculars. This was a spot where European Golden Plovers had been seen in previous years

Alice Approves of a Snow Crab

in April. I had seldom, if ever, found rare vagrant birds on my own and, therefore, lacked confidence. Finally, after more than an hour of scouring the area, I noticed some movement in the grass; it was well camouflaged, but I got close enough to get the bird in my glasses. I confirmed all the markings of a breeding-plumage European Golden Plover, the only one reported in North America that year, and my first rarity found entirely by myself. I had put myself in a position to make this discovery by "doing my homework," words heard ad nauseam from my prophetic and demanding parents of blessed memory who, like me, were lobster-and-crab-eating Jews.

I rushed back to the cabin and insisted that my wife and friends come to verify what otherwise might have been a hallucination. They easily saw, identified, and photographed this bird, the name of which now sits proudly in its proper place on my life list of birds seen in North America.

European Golden Plover. Notice the Extensive White on its Flanks,
Which both American and Pacific Golden Plovers Lack

There are three species of Golden Plover. The Pacific Golden Plover nests in Alaska and the eastern Arctic. It has dark underwings and less white on its flanks. I have seen this in breeding plumage in Alaska in the company of Whimbrels and Bristle-thighed Curlews. It is more commonly seen wintering on the golf courses of Hawaii, where an otherwise intelligent medical colleague who spent several years of his career in Hawaii referred to them as "ploovers." I'm not certain what a "ploover" is, but I am certain that it cannot fly and is more likely to be found in a bar than on a golf course. The other common Golden Plover of North America is the more centrally located American Golden Plover, commonly seen migrating through Nova Scotia. That bird has no white on its flanks and is a smaller, stockier bird with a shorter bill, which causes it to arrive at its destination slightly later than birds with longer bills.

Of course, there is always some darkness with the light; in this case, five days after we departed, a small flock of Black-tailed Godwits was found in the same area where I found the plover. I have yet to see that bird. On the other hand, I did find a Eurasian Hobby, a small falcon rarely seen in North America, in the same area as the plover. This was a great surprise and another life bird.

During this trip, Alice also became pregnant with her first child—apparently, the newlyweds enjoyed Newfoundland. The blessed event more than compensated for the missed Black-tailed Godwits. As for me, the wildness of Newfoundland and the appeal of the avian rarities of northern latitudes would soon beckon me to Alaska, a gold mine of birds, bears, and extremes, the last North American frontier.

Arctic Loon

Cara-bus in Nome

ALASKA: A BIRDER'S LAST FRONTIER

Alaska, one of the most remote regions of North America and the region closest to Asia, is a mecca for birders who wish to maximize their sightings in North America. Most of the birds of Alaska are found near water, either in Alaskan coastal locations such as Homer, Nome, and Barrow, or far out to sea on several islands in the Aleutian and Bering Seas. These islands attract a wide variety of Asian vagrants that are seldom seen elsewhere. One exception is the Grey-headed Tit, perhaps the most difficult bird to see on the ABA list. The bird is found deep in the interior and requires a long raft trip for a chance to see it. Unfortunately, it hasn't been found in the last few years and might be extinct in the Western Hemisphere. If that is true, I believe I have seen all the indigenous nesting birds of North America.

NOME, ALASKA IN LATE SPRING

RULE 21
Again, our upright posture separates us from the apes,
so for Darwin's sake, and your own, keep on walking.

I booked my first birding trip to Alaska in early June 2009. My destinations were St. Paul Island and Nome. Nome is located on the west coast of Alaska, about an hour's flight north of Anchorage. It is a quaint town with friendly people anxious to provide service to travelers. It marks the finish line of the iconic Iditarod Trail Sled Dog Race. Nome has one main restaurant, Milano's Pizza.

Nome also has extensive wetlands along the open ocean, estuaries, and bays, which provide great shorebird opportunities. The water, including the ocean, is frozen in winter when Polar bears occasionally appear on the ice sheet.

The town is unconnected to other Alaskan cities except by air or boat, but it has three roads that extend northeast, east, or southeast about 100 miles out into the tundra. Along these roads are rivers, lakes, hills, and a few stands of boreal forest. The rivers are littered with old gold-mining structures, some still in use. It is noteworthy that one of the roads ends at a riverbank with a small village on the other side, while another ends at a bridge with nothing on the other side. Go figure; it's Alaska.

In summer, Nome can produce oddities, but the main goal is to see the predictable but locally restricted birds like the Arctic Warbler, Bluethroat, Arctic Loon, Aleutian Tern, three species of ptarmigan, and, most importantly, the Bristle-thighed Curlew. The latter is predictably found on top of a hill that requires a moderate climb and is located at mile 72 from Nome on the northeastern road. Perhaps not surprisingly, this hill is known as Curlew Hill. Curlew Hill, also known as Coffee Dome, is the only reliable place to find breeding Bristle-thighed Curlews without getting off-road and into grizzly bear territory, but it is not only home to the Bristle-thighed Curlew. The more *abundant* Whimbrel and many exquisite Pacific Golden Plovers can be found there too. Moreover, in early summer the tundra is just beginning to bloom, so the climb provides much more to see and admire than the birds.

The Bristle-thighed Curlew can be found occasionally wintering in Hawaii, which is indicative of high intelligence.

For our first outing, we headed out with some urgency just after arrival to find singing Bluethroats, since this bird, having completed its mating ritual, was about to leave its territory and disappear in silence into the wilderness. We were fortunate to find one and see its stunning throat, which is blue with rufous and black stripes. We also found an Arctic Warbler before getting some nutrition and sleep. The next day was our first long trip northeast toward our main goal, Curlew Hill.

On the way to Curlew Hill, we spotted Willow Ptarmigan and Rock Ptarmigan and found a Gyrfalcon nesting on a bridge. We passed a grizzly bear along the road, which skulked off into the willows. There were musk oxen around, as well as sporadic caribou. We found many nesting species of interest, including Jaegers, Wheatears, Rock Sandpipers, and Lapland Longspurs, all in striking breeding plumage.

The Rock Sandpiper is the western counterpart of the previously described Purple Sandpiper of the Northeast coast.

However, when we arrived at Curlew Hill and prepared for the trek to the top, one of our flock—a visibly vigorous and not elderly woman, who was the spouse of another member of the group—declared that she would stay in the car.

"I have no intention of climbing that hill," she said with conviction. "You can't see 'em all."

I was startled by her decision and continue to be confused by it. Why travel so far for this unique opportunity and then decline it? I suspected either a domestic dispute or some physical problem that wasn't apparent. There are, however, some people for whom the most trivial level of physical discomfort or exertion is simply intolerable. Such people will circle grocery store parking lots numerous times to avoid walking a few extra feet. In any case, this nice lady, who seemed perfectly pleasant in every other way, did not ascend Curlew Hill with the rest of us.

Bristle-thighed Curlew

Curlew Hill Tundra
in Early Summer

This episode troubled me. Perhaps she had a good reason, but I was sorry that she missed out on such a wondrous experience: We easily located the prized bird as well as a spate of stunning Pacific Golden Plovers in breeding plumage, something seldom seen during migration when this species is most frequently found. The Bristle-thighed Curlews were less numerous than the other curlews, Whimbrels, which are less ruddy and have whiter tails. Despite the tendency for birders to be loners, there is great joy in sharing special moments like these with others.

It also wasn't just the target bird that our reluctant companion missed out on: Although I had enjoyed some of the same spectacular flora in Colorado's High Rocky Mountains, I had never seen tundra this far north before. It was stunning. Birders, whose eyes are usually focused on trees, bushes, or the sky, often miss things on the ground, and I have made a point since I was in Nome to always observe the ground under my feet. (Being aware of the ground also reduces the chance of stepping on a snake or in a hole and rupturing an Achilles tendon, as I did a few years earlier—something I don't recommend unless you want to walk like a duck.)

On the long drive back to Nome, we looked for the grizzly that we had seen on the way and found it sleeping peacefully, perhaps 500 feet above us on a steep rocky cliff. Dave McKay stopped the car, got out, and yelled, "Hey bear!!!" at the top of his lungs. The bear sat up and stared at us for a few seconds, shook itself, and went back to sleep. We had a good laugh, partly at Dave's antics and partly at our insignificance, so clearly demonstrated by the great beast peacefully napping above us.

The experience at Curlew Hill was the highlight of the trip, but a great view of an Arctic Loon in breeding plumage was a close second. The loons, in general, are among my favorite birds. They are elegant in their lines, with just enough color and pattern to enhance their shape. From a painter's perspective, loons are a nearly perfect subject. I remembered my heartbreaking near miss of seeing an Arctic Loon in Denver, far from its normal territory, when I arrived seconds after the spooked bird had disappeared. Seeing the loon in its comfort zone and in breeding plumage more than made up for the miss in Denver. It never fails to amaze me how virtually every negative, sooner or later, is turned into a positive. This, of course, applies to everything in life. As a neuro-oncologist, a brain tumor doctor, I have lost many patients, but those few cured patients were more than enough reward to keep me going for decades.

As for the positives, this trip to Nome gave me my first taste of Alaska, including the eclectic food at Milano's Pizza.

I savored both.

RULE 22
If you see a penguin north of the equator, consult your
eye doctor and/or your psychiatrist; if the bird is not a
hallucination, it is most likely a puffin.

The second and highly anticipated stop on my June trip to Alaska was St. Paul Island in the Bering Sea, where we were certain to see a panoply of nesting alcids, penguin-like seabirds. We soon found ourselves airborne for our bumpy flight.

We stayed in a large complex that provides hearty cafeteria-style meals and comfortable rooms. As is required, we were accompanied on all our excursions by a lovely and competent young woman of Indigenous ancestry, whose cheerful demeanor was endearing. She and our leader hit it off, and we enjoyed their constant banter about life in Alaska.

We scoured the island and, in the process, saw all its diverse avian denizens. We easily found Bar-tailed Godwits in a pond near the compound. A trip to the cliffs, which provide safe nesting for thousands of seabirds, offered views of Horned and Tufted Puffins, as well as many auklets, including Least, Crested, and Parakeet. Those two puffins, along with the Atlantic Puffin, are the northern answer to penguins, which, despite a few notorious cartoons, are seen only south of the equator. We found and were dazzled by Red-legged Kittiwakes, one of the most striking North American gulls, and very different from the Black-legged Kittiwakes I saw in Witless Bay, Newfoundland. St. Paul Island is the only reliable place to see Red-legged Kittiwakes, which are uniquely neckless, with a short, greenish bill that complements the brilliant red legs. We also found Red-faced Cormorants, which look like they have had a few too many nightcaps.

We spent considerable time searching various productive locations for rarities and found a few, including a flock of spectacular Emperor Geese in full breeding plumage. Some rare birds that had been reported eluded our group, but no one cared in the end—we were too engaged with studying, photographing, and simply enjoying the accessible menagerie of nesting seabirds. Our trusty leader came down with a head cold but soldiered on and accompanied us back to Anchorage.

Tufted Puffin

Horned Puffin

Emperor Goose Below, Long-Tailed Duck Above, with Palette Abstract

NOME ALASKA IN WINTER:
MCKAY'S BUNTING AND A BROTHEL CHICKADEE

When I made my first visit to Nome with Dave MacKay, I asked about McKay's Bunting (no relationship), a small, mostly-white seedeater that nests only on a few inaccessible islands in the Bering Sea but migrates to the "greener pastures" of coastal Alaska in winter. Because of that, relatively few birders have seen it. Furthermore, I had never seen any organized trips offered to see this bird—there is little else to justify a trip to Nome in winter. Dave had told me that residents of Nome find these buntings on their feeders in winter. This was encouraging, but despite many inquiries and calls, I could not confirm anyone who would verify the presence of the bird; without that confirmation, I would not take the long and expensive flight.

Finally, in 2018, I discovered a guide who lives in Homer and guides exclusively in Alaska (with the exception of an annual trip to Cambodia). His company has numerous Alaskan excursions, including a winter trip to Nome in search of McKay's Bunting. He also offers a fall trip to Barrow to see the Ross's Gull migration. I was able to get the last spot for the bunting trip. I knew this was the only way that I would ever see this bird, considered to be the whitest songbird in the world. I would have another life bird and belong to an elite group of inveterate birders who had seen it. We also had the opportunity for encounters with polar bear, wolves, and other rare wintering birds.

The trip to Nome goes through Anchorage, where we gathered and spent the night. Flying into Anchorage in late winter daylight is almost worth the trip by itself. Denali can be seen if it is not cloud-covered, and the snowy terrain and frozen water are spectacular. The morning flight to Nome also provided amazing views. We landed safely and were soon trudging around town, where birdseed had been spread to attract the buntings. Within minutes, we had spotted the birds perched on wires and feeding on the ground. They were in the company of many Snow Buntings, which ordinarily would be difficult to distinguish, but we had plenty of time and the

McKay's Bunting

Snow Bunting (L) and
McKay's Bunting (R)

joy of noticing every detail. Without the seed, we would have been searching the grassy shores for miles to spot these birds and might not have been successful, but the residents of Nome are mindful of this rare winter visitor and the more common Snow Buntings. They would feed the avian winter visitors anyway but are happy to host a few serious birders and appreciate their contribution to the local economy.

We noted that the McKay's Bunting has less black and ruddy color on its back, wings, and tail than the Snow Bunting, and is close to pure white. It has black feet and eyes, which stand out against the white, and a thick orange bill. Much to our enjoyment, we could also hear it sing; these birds are in breeding mode in March—I guess they thought it was spring, all things, as Einstein said, being relative. During our two days in Nome, we made several appearances in town to live with our buntings and never lost interest. (Even if we had, there was nothing else to do.)

During our time in Nome, we also heard about some wolves that were spotted near a local farm, approximately ten miles from town. We set out to see them, but the road became treacherous and signs ominously warned us not to go further or to face the consequences. Alaskans are good at rescuing but strive to avoid it, especially when the cause is human stupidity. We obeyed the signs: no rescue, but also no wolves. We did, however, drive the plowed roads for a few hours and found a pair of Gyrfalcons, many Willow Ptarmigan, and a Boreal Chickadee visiting a feeder at the town brothel—accordingly, we renamed it Brothel Chickadee.

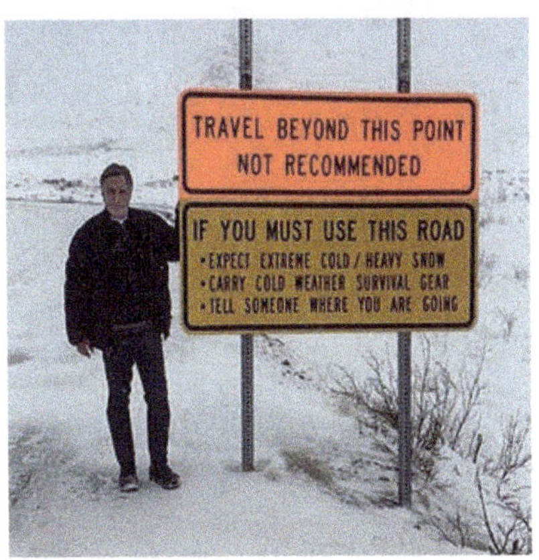

Your Author, One Man Who
Follows Directions

Boreal Chickadee on
Feeder at Nome Brothel

Willow Ptarmigan

And so, McKay's Bunting now lives with my other listed birds in a position of high importance, earned by its beauty, remoteness, and cooperativeness, which brought together a hardy group of birders under the leadership of an excellent guide.

Non-birders might ask why we went so far to see this bird. The answer is, in part, to be asked that question and have the opportunity to reply: "Because it had feathers and it was there."

Eastern Black Rail

NEW BERN, NORTH CAROLINA, AND THE CROATAN NATIONAL FOREST

RULE 24
A frustrating irony is to search for something in futility,
then find it when you are not looking for it.
(But if you expect to find things by not looking
for them, you are throwing moss at a glass house.)

In 2006, I went on a family vacation to the Outer Banks of North Carolina with my two younger children, Robin and Patty, my daughter Rebecca, and my second wife Julie. We had done this before, and I had taken the opportunity to get out into the Gulf Stream for pelagic birds, once on a fishing charter and once on an organized trip out of Oregon Inlet. These trips, in addition to a touch of seasickness, produced looks at several great birds, including Cory's Shearwater, Greater Shearwater, Black-capped Petrel, Herald Petrel, Audubon's Shearwater, Yellow-billed Tropicbird (now known as White-tailed Tropicbird), and Band-rumped Storm Petrel —also a gorgeous yellowfin tuna that we feasted on for days. (The tuna was caught by Rebecca, who was brave enough to join me.)

In 2007, instead of venturing into the Gulf Stream, I made plans to travel to the southern part of North Carolina, near historic New Bern, the first capital of the state and the birthplace of Pepsi. I had found someone there who was well known for locating Eastern Black Rails in the coastal marsh, the only nesting rail that I had not seen and a very difficult bird to find, even in its prime territory.

I didn't realize that to get from northern to southern North Carolina, one must drive hundreds of miles on meandering roads to get around the incursions of water that block the more direct route along the coast.

In truth, the drive was an opportunity to get acquainted with the remnants of the Antebellum South by car. A lot of it looks like it hasn't changed much since the days of tobacco and slavery, with people sitting fanning themselves on porches, countless Purple Martin houses, magnolias, and Spanish moss. The downside was that I was afraid I would be late for our planned attempt to wade into the marsh at dusk, when the circumstances were optimal to see the Eastern Black Rail. Somehow, I managed to reach the appointed place on time without any interruption from the highway patrol.

My guide and I headed for the saw grass marsh, after a generous dousing of insect repellent, donning disposable shoes since the black muck has the habit of swallowing them. We followed a well-trodden path with numerous species of marsh birds holding forth as they tend to do as the sun approaches the horizon. We soon heard the characteristic repeating call of the rail, "kic kee der."

We responded electronically, which my guide reassured me would excite but not disturb the bird. Often, these rails will not show themselves, and birders must settle for a sound-only identification. There was no doubt we had heard our bird, but what we didn't expect was the Eastern Black Rail bursting out of the foliage, flying within inches of our noses, then diving back into the seclusion of the marsh. It has been several years since this experience, but it feels like it happened yesterday. Aware as I now am of the precarious state of this rail, I am less comfortable with our use of a tape to lure it out of its cover. In general, I feel tapes should be avoided, but when they work, the results can be spectacular.

We trudged triumphantly back to the car, where I expressed my most sincere appreciation for this thrill, and then I returned to my motel for some rest. I had an early morning departure with another local birder to explore an area in the Croatan National Forest.

I met my next birding guide at dawn, and we drove a short distance to a place that held much more than I expected. We first succeeded in viewing singing Bachman's Sparrows, a drab bird with a very loud and musical song that begins with a sustained single note followed by a high-pitched trill.

This sparrow sighting got me closer to my goal of seeing all the breeding sparrows of North America—I was only missing Le Conte's, Nelson's, and Baird's, all of which I have since seen.

While enjoying this bird and studying its subtle field marks, I heard rapid knocking and looked up to see rare Red-cockaded Woodpeckers, which appeared to be nesting in the first-growth loblolly pines that surrounded us. I had seen this bird before, after hours of hiking around a stand of old loblolly pines south of Augusta, Georgia. On this day, no such effort was required.

This can be a common experience in birding: You work very hard to find something, and then, on another occasion, it just appears. It reminds me of couples who spend thousands of dollars to get pregnant and then get pregnant again the traditional way. I'm not sure what the lesson is, but I'm sure there is one. Either it's that all hard work is eventually rewarded, or that hard work is foolish, and one should simply wait with patience for the problem to solve itself.

The Croatan National Forest of North Carolina is unique more for its flora than its fauna. Although I am not a botanist, I do enjoy being with people who are. I always learn something and frequently see amazing things. This was one of those times. The forest is home to at least five species of carnivorous plants and several rare orchids. I was able to see many of these with the help of my knowledgeable guide. I also learned that the Venus Flytraps one can purchase are virtually all derived from the resident natural population of this area. I was moved to write a poem:

Venus Flytrap

tasty white flowers
above
yellowed grass

insects
overloaded with pollen
fall

Venus Flytraps
unseen
wait below

OKLAHOMA AND THE LONGSPURS
OF NORTH AMERICA

Let me turn now to the subject of longspurs. They are chunky, long-winged, seed-eating birds that are ground dwellers. They get their name from a long claw that protrudes backward from their foot. There are four species, although one, McCown's Longspur, has been moved to a separate genus and renamed Thick-billed Longspur. The others are Chestnut-collared, Lapland, and Smith's Longspurs. None are easily found, as the birds are relatively scarce and favor remote locations. I have been fortunate to see all four species.

I went on a field trip in the early 1970s with the Denver Field Ornithologists to the Pawnee National Grasslands. This is a tract of preserved short-grass prairie, north of Denver and east of Greeley, which is home to innumerable Lark Buntings, the state bird of Colorado. It is also the best place in Colorado to find both Thick-billed and Chestnut-collared Longspurs. The males of these species have the unusual behavior during the breeding season of lifting briefly off the ground to sing their mating song and then parachuting back into the grass. This enables them to be located by the females—and by birders like us. These two species are seldom found together since the Thick-billed prefers areas of sparse vegetation, whereas the Chestnut-collared prefers denser grass. But the Pawnee National Grassland has both, and a trip there also might include Pawnee Buttes, where there are nesting Prairie Falcons. The wildflowers can be spectacular after a snowy winter.

My next longspur was the Lapland, which I found in winter in Colorado in a large flock of Horned Larks, the usual way of finding the Lapland Larkspur. The bird is identifiable primarily by its black tail outlined with white edges. When I saw it again years later in Alaska, it was as handsome as I remembered.

Finally, the Smith's Longspur—my last and most challenging. It breeds in northern Canada and Alaska, but it's possible to see during

Smith's Longspur

migration, as it winters in the central United States and southern Canada. Again, the tail is key: Smith's Longspur has a whiter tail than the Lapland.

Enter: Oklahoma.

I had known for some time that Smith's Longspur was often present in Oklahoma in winter and reported in Christmas bird counts, but I had never had an opportunity to look for it. In 2010, I was invited by a former colleague, Dr. Nancy Cersonsky, in early spring to give a talk about my brain tumor research at the new Proton Beam Radiation Center in Oklahoma City. I accepted the opportunity and started looking for someone who might know how to find the longspurs.

I was very lucky to find a woman named Naomi Swift on an online platform called Birding Pal. Naomi was one of those "characters" you come across when you are looking for friendly and accommodating birders. She'd been part of the impressive group of women birders from Oklahoma that I had met on my trip to the Dry Tortugas years earlier. The longspurs, she told me, were wintering close to the hospital where I was going to present my talk.

After my talk, I met Naomi and a friend who had space for me in a high-clearance SUV. We traveled to a vacant lot situated in a mixed residential and commercial area within the city limits of Oklahoma City. My guide proceeded to drive the SUV into this grassy lot and erratically zig-zag through the field. A few minutes later, as I was watching for the police, a flock of birds rose briefly and settled again on the ground. We jumped out of the vehicle and spread out as we walked toward the area where we had seen the birds. Soon, we found and identified a flock of Smith's Longspurs, some of which had some of the striking facial markings of breeding plumage.

Of course, I was thrilled. I took the two women to lunch, during which Naomi's friend told me that her spouse had the dicey job of chasing wall clouds during tornado season and was gone for months until the season ended. Tornadoes have always fascinated me. I thought about asking if I could join her husband, but managed to stifle this foolish impulse. Certainly, the day had been a surreal experience, one of my most memorable, and a better place to end this chapter than inside a tornado.

I had seen all the longspurs of North America.

BRITISH COLUMBIA:
A REDWING IN THE HOLLY

RULE 26
There is much to be learned from
the young if you are not.

In January 2017, I discovered that a Redwing, a stray European thrush, was consistently found (albeit with some difficulty) in a giant holly growth in Victoria, British Columbia. I monitored this situation, hoping something else might pop up. Sure enough, a Siberian Accentor showed up on a farm north of Vancouver. It would be possible to see two new birds in a beautiful area with only a ferry ride needed to negotiate the water between the sites. Additionally, I welcomed any excuse to visit British Columbia, and especially Victoria.

The Redwing is a common thrush in its natural European habitat. It shows up occasionally in the Canadian Maritimes, but rarely on the West Coast. The Siberian Accentor is a common bird in Asia that appears unpredictably during its migration to the American islands near Siberia, including Adak and Gamble. I was able to get a direct flight from Denver to Victoria, and off I went.

I arrived in time to make a run to the Redwing site before dusk. When I got there, I was told that the Redwing had been seen in the last hour, but had the frustrating habit of disappearing into the dense holly for hours and then popping out briefly. Since darkness was upon us, I decided to call it a night and rise early, hoping to see the bird in time to make the ferry to North Vancouver and try for the Siberian Accentor.

I arrived early with other birders in a cold, persistent drizzle. We set up shop and waited… and waited, and waited. Many people out walking in their suburban neighborhood asked about the fuss; as usual, they were incredulous that people from so many places would be there to see this little thrush. Eventually, the bird made an appearance with little enthusiasm for the dreary weather. I just caught a glance in my glasses, but a young, rising-star birder next to me named Liron Gertsman—maybe 16 years old at the time— caught the bird with a very large lens and texted me a photo, shown here. It shows the Redwing's striking facial and throat markings and its bicolored bill.

This was the best look anybody had that day, and the bird disappeared a few days later. Without this photo, I would not be certain of what I had seen. There is no question that the approach of using a zoom lens or scope with a camera mount has become the way to go for better bird identification. I was very lucky that this young man was willing to share his photo. We corresponded briefly afterward but lost track. As expected, Liron has become a star birder in the birdy areas of western Canada. And I have taken up photography, although some might disagree with calling me a photographer. This was a fortuitous nexus of the new, technically proficient breed of birders and the old guard.

After my brief glimpse of the Redwing, I headed for the ferry port and arrived on time. We had a pleasant voyage to the mainland ferry port, where there is a large garbage dump that attracts hundreds of Bald Eagles. I had never seen anything like it before, but my target was the Accentor, so I didn't linger and used GPS to find the remote farm where it had been showing up.

Once I found the property, I stood around the site listening to stories of the bird's erratic behavior and exact whereabouts during the previous sightings. I spent several hours there, but the bird didn't show up and was never reported again. I had some time to spend with the eagles on the way back to Victoria Island. I had missed one rare bird but found another and witnessed an incredible display of bald eagles.

Not bad.

This wasn't my first birding adventure in British Columbia.

Back in 2015, I hiked the West Coast Trail of Vancouver Island with several friends. Although it was late September, the weather was shockingly warm, and the unusual array of avian fauna reflected this phenomenon—Brown Pelicans were flying along the shore hundreds of miles north of their usual range. Apparently these conditions were caused by an El Niño, a weather phenomenon characterized by unusually warm water, a harbinger of the climate changes we are now experiencing.

At the end of our first day's hike, about ten miles south of the north trailhead at Port Renfrew, we were hot and tired and decided, against our better judgment, to take a swim in the usually chilly waters of Vancouver Island. Once in the water, we realized it was warm enough to stay in and enjoy, not just get a brief rinse. We were quickly joined by a family of Harlequin Ducks that probably had never encountered humans in the water. They were unafraid, very curious, and provided

Harlequin Ducks

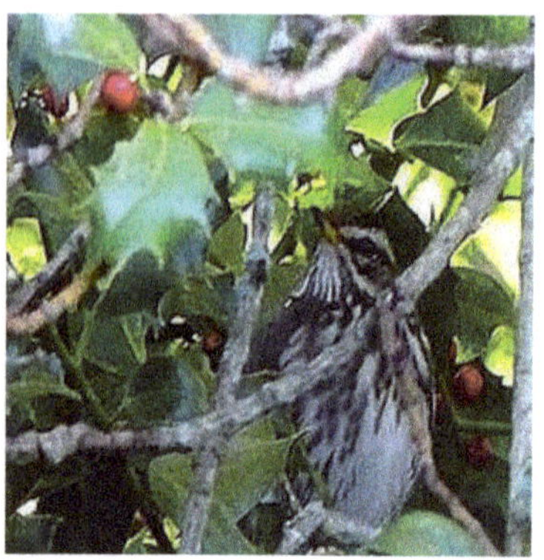

Redwing in Holly - Photograph
Provided by Liron Gertsman

us with a great thrill as they circled us while softly commenting to each other on our strange presence. The Harlequin is one of the more striking ducks in the world, and despite the ominous warning of the El Niño phenomenon, we were all thrilled, including my non-birder hiking buddies.

For anyone who enjoys spectacular scenery, the West Coast Trail is a must. The best section of the Trail is along the northern half, which is mostly on the beach, where a limestone shelf provides easy hiking with constant views of spouting grey whales, sea lions, eagles, and other bird life. The trail goes perhaps 50 miles south, and many hikers shuttle from the end back to their cars. I have always made a U-turn at about the halfway point, where the trail goes deep into the humid and muddy rainforest with few opportunities to walk along the ocean. To cross a series of raging torrents running to the sea, it is necessary to load your heavy pack and yourself onto the equivalent of a roller coaster seat after climbing a slippery ladder, then launch yourself over the water on a cable to reach the other side without drowning. It is exhilarating and as unforgettable as the scenery, but not for everybody.

When we returned to Victoria, we spent at least an hour getting enough mud off our bodies to look more like humans than yetis. The next day, we went on an excursion to see orcas, which we were fortunate enough to find. The first sighting of these creatures with their huge dorsal fins exceeds all expectations. I have seen many whales during my birding adventures at sea, but I had never seen an orca. These huge and highly intelligent carnivores inspire awe in the

West Coast Trail, Vancouver Island   Ruff

wild that is, in my experience, unmatched. Who needs science fiction when reality is so powerful?

The following day, I found myself alone, as my fellow hikers had departed. I was aware of the presence of a Ruff along the Victoria waterfront. I had never seen this uncommon shorebird, which is an irregular visitor from Eurasia. I walked about a mile along the shore of Puget Sound with some protest from my hiker's legs, but managed to find the bird, my only sighting to date.

This large sandpiper shows lots of red on its face and nape, which contrasts with its dark, scalloped back. When it is in breeding plumage in Europe, the male is adorned with outlandish plumes on its head, for obvious reasons.

British Columbia is a vast and magnificent corner of North America. I have been privileged to visit it several times, and, as always, to enhance the experience with some of its spectacular feathered inhabitants. Other lifers for me in B.C. are Eurasian Skylark and Sharp-tailed Sandpiper.

PART 5

THE QUEST

**I RETIRE, ESCAPE TO CANADA,
AND LAUNCH MY QUEST**

RULE 27
Aversion to risk carries the risk of squandering benefits.

On March 16, 2020, we pulled away from the gate into Canada, took deep breaths, and looked at each other. We had made it. The sense of relief we felt is difficult to describe, like a skydiver on his first jump when the parachute opens. Now we could make our long journey to Cape Breton, 5,600 kilometers away, with peace of mind.

In 2014, my wife, Aura, and I went to Nova Scotia on vacation. We had never been there but had heard of its remarkable beauty and culture. We planned to arrive in Halifax and then drive to Cape Breton Island, the easternmost part of the Province. We would spend some time taking in the local Scottish and Acadian cultures, then work our way to western Nova Scotia, the Annapolis Valley, and back to Halifax.

Northern Ontario Near Thunder Bay,
March 17, 2020

However, we fell in love with Cape Breton and never left until it was time to go to Halifax and fly home. It might have been the glorious autumn colors, or the energy of the international *Celtic Colours* music festival taking place during our visit. But somehow, Aura and I found ourselves deciding this might be a place to settle and contacted a local realtor, Sherry MacLeod, who lubricated us with some excellent local spirits and showed us some affordable properties. She also got us tickets to a couple of *Celtic Colours* concerts, which were mesmerizing.

By the time we departed, we had resolved to purchase a property in Cape Breton.

In 2018, Sherry found us the perfect house, and we simply couldn't turn down the opportunity, We took possession a year later in the autumn of 2019. Our plan was to spend time in both Denver and Cape Breton. Once we moved in, we discovered that Cape Breton was a unique place that reminded us of Alice in Wonderland, where things get "curiouser and curiouser." This arrangement set the table for our unexpected migration to Canada in March 2020, to sit out the pandemic and the first Trumpian dystopia.

As the year 2020 began, my vision was no longer 20/20, and I was approaching my 75th birthday. Otherwise, things seemed normal, or normally abnormal. I made a quick opportunistic run to Arizona, where I located my first Rufous-backed Robin, an annual vagrant from Mexico that I needed for my life list.

Aura and I visited Cape Breton in February 2020 to check whether our new home was comfortable during winter and to prepare

Vagrant: Also called an accidental which presumes that the bird has no reason to be where it is. Owners of parrots should teach their pets to recite their address if asked by a birder. I had been a frequent visitor to Arizona in search of rare birds. Little did I know that the pandemic would keep me away for nearly three years and cost me several rarities that were high on my "must-see" list. This robin from south of the border was my only consolation.

it for our planned summer stay. Shortly after we returned to Denver, we began hearing about a novel and virulent respiratory virus in China. On Friday, March 13, I ran into one of my colleagues, Dr. Mary Laird Warner, director of the intensive care unit at Swedish Medical Center, where I was working in wound care and hyperbaric medicine, as well as seeing my brain tumor patients. Mary told me the hospital was filling rapidly with patients who were critically ill with the novel Coronavirus. She looked me in the eye and stated emphatically, "Ed, you should leave the hospital now and not return. You are at very high risk based on your age and your asthma. The Coronavirus patients are desperately ill, and we have no effective treatment."

I took this seriously; Mary is a fine physician and a friend. But was this really the end of my five-decade-long career as a healer? It had become my identity and provided me with a much-needed sense of "being of use."

The phrase "being of use" is borrowed from the book The Cider House Rules by John Irving. In that novel, Dr. Wilbur Larch, the protagonist, repeatedly understates his passion as "being of use."

My forced retirement came at a time when I had just discovered that oxygen under pressure, hyperbaric oxygen, could repair the vascular damage done by radiation to the brains of brain tumor survivors, of which I had many. The lost opportunity to continue this research made an abrupt life change even more traumatic.

When I got home, I was greeted by Aura, who asked with skepticism: "Is this it? You're not going back?" I wasn't certain if this was a real question or a command, but it was clear that she agreed with

Rufous-backed Robin

my decision. We quickly made a plan to seek refuge from the virus at our home in Canada. It would take some time for the adrenaline rush of fleeing to Canada to subside enough for me to fully comprehend the immensity of this moment.

I figured we could take a few days to get ready for our trip since we would be driving; flights were too risky. Aura disagreed and insisted that we leave early Sunday morning. That gave us one day to get ready. We contacted our Canadian immigration attorney, who advised us to minimize our luggage and bring documents to prove that we were American citizens with property and bank accounts in the United States, so we would be correctly perceived as visitors to Canada. There was concern about how we would be regarded by the Canadian Border Control, which we would encounter in Pembina, Manitoba, the closest crossing to Colorado. Our anxiety was high as we began our journey.

We departed in our trusty all-track Volkswagen Tiguan at 5 a.m. on Sunday, March 15, 2020, with a loaded cooler of food and drinks, and headed for Grand Forks, North Dakota, just south of the Canadian border. We were relieved to be on our way to a safer place where we had seen no evidence of pandemic denial. We were shocked by the desultory response in the United States to this enormously dangerous virus. However, three years of Donald Trump had taught us to expect the worst. I was sad to leave many patients in limbo, but I knew they would understand, and I could work with them remotely. We would also be separated indefinitely from our six children and four grandchildren, who would remain in the United States.

Our route took us through the Sand Hills country of Nebraska, then along the Missouri River Valley into Iowa and the Dakotas. Fortunately, the weather was accommodating and the flocks of Horned Larks and Snow Geese, indifferent to the burgeoning pandemic, gave us some peace of mind. My passion for birds and birding has always provided me with comfort in challenging times. We arrived at our motel in Grand Forks about 13 hours later, just as it began to snow. I chose to eat something in the dining room, which was ominously empty, but Aura more wisely chose to stay in our hotel room. We had begun our new life of pandemic precautions and restrictions.

We left at dawn the next morning to arrive at customs early, as advised, with a fresh crew of officers who were less likely to be grumpy. As we exited the motel lot, we were held up by the world's longest freight train, the caboose of which was probably still somewhere in South Dakota as the engine first passed us. We arrived at Pembina in Manitoba around 9 a.m., an hour later than we had planned. As we slowly approached the Canadian Border Security booth, our collective pulse and blood pressure rose. We knew we were at risk of being turned back, but our lawyer was on call if we needed help. Our customs officer was a young woman, pleasant but humorless, and not interested in pleasantries. She asked about our destination, our reason for traveling to Canada, and our Coronavirus exposure history. She also asked, of course, about symptoms. We answered all her questions honestly, and she let us pass without further ado.

We knew we had made the right decision to leave the United States quickly, and that we had been a little lucky and a lot smart to have taken the "road less traveled" by purchasing our home in Cape Breton, without which we could not have fled to the relative safety of Canada. Between my approaching 75th birthday and my worsening asthma after a bout with influenza, I might not have survived a case of Coronavirus. I would be much safer in an isolated rural environment and in a country where Trump was not president.

The next afternoon, March 17, St. Patrick's Day, my friend Buzz called from California to let us know the United States-Canada border was closed. We had dodged a bullet. It had taken the better part of 50 years, two-thirds of my life, to reach a sense of usefulness and meaning through my work. I had left it behind, just as Aura, also a skilled healthcare professional, had left her work behind. I would need to rediscover myself, but the task at hand dominated my thoughts.

We drove that day to Thunder Bay, a place that does not live up to its lyrical name, even though it does have a bay and, undoubtedly, thunder. We noticed that appropriate measures were already in effect

Winston, our Guardian Bald Eagle, Watches from his Perch

in Canada to control the virus. We saw fear in the eyes of those who noticed our American license plates and were appropriately concerned about Trump's nonchalance and denial of the pandemic.

From Thunder Bay, we elected to take a northern route through Ontario to avoid large cities. We stayed in Timmins after driving hundreds of miles without seeing any signs for food or fuel. Everything was covered with snow, and the lakes were frozen. It was the Great White North, but the weather cooperated. The long journey was surreal and, especially for Jews like us, recalled the Exodus from Egypt, although there was no need to eat locusts. Instead, there was poutine.

When we finally reached Fredericton, New Brunswick, four days after crossing the US-Canadian border, we knew we would make it to Cape Breton the next day. We phoned Sherry MacLeod, our former realtor turned friend, to let her know our status. We collected some food along the way whenever possible so we would have something to eat when we arrived. Who knew if the stores were open or what they had to sell? We drove by a Walmart in Moncton but decided to avoid the long lines. The world had changed.

We arrived in McNabs Cove late in the afternoon of March 20, 2020, and found a care package on the doorstep left by Sherry containing food and some other staples. That is the Cape Breton way. We felt welcome and relieved, full of gratitude and even joy to be in this sanctuary despite knowing that the future was uncertain. We notified our children that we had arrived safely, ate something, climbed into our warm bed, and passed out. This journey had ended well, and we looked forward to a new life in a new land.

We awoke to the squawks of wintering geese and the watchful eye of our resident Bald Eagle, Winston. Despite many uncertainties, we were safely isolated in a new land. Birding, which had been a therapeutic avocation for me for five decades, could, in the absence of a medical practice, become a full-time passion, a *raison d'etre.*

NOVA SCOTIA:
NEARING A MAJOR MILESTONE

When I arrived in Cape Breton in 2020, after my narrow escape from the COVID pandemic, I was aware that I would have some birding opportunities. I was, quite abruptly, retired and now living in a place uniquely different from anywhere I had lived before. I had spent the previous 32 years living and working in Colorado, where I first took up birding. While Colorado is blessed with a rich avifauna, it is not a magnet for rarities compared to Florida, Texas, California, and Arizona. Northeastern North America can be added to that list, and here I was, an inhabitant, not a visitor, in the boreal forest that extends northward to the tundra and is never far from water. I was living with an abundance of birds that many birders, including me, would endure considerable expense and privations to find. At the time, I had no inkling of how dramatically this would affect my life as a birder. Seeing uncommon birds is one thing; having them as your neighbors during the isolation of a pandemic is another thing altogether.

My first birding experience in Nova Scotia was with Billy Digout, a Cape Breton Renaissance man—teacher, surveyor, trapper, church organist, and bingo captain—who was gracious enough, once we made contact in April 2020, to invite me to join him for a survey of owl nesting boxes that he had put up in forests near St. Peters. These boxes were designed to attract a tiny species of owl, the Northern Saw-whet Owl, which is common here but seldom seen. I had already been out at night listening for them without success. Since the birds are widely scattered, it helps to know where to look, and as I had heard many Saw-whets but never actually seen one, this was a great opportunity.

We met one morning in early spring and set out for the forest surrounding Corbet's Cove, which is typical of the southern coast of Bras d'Or Lake, an inland sea that divides Cape Breton in half from

Barred Owl

Northern Saw-Whet Owl in Billy's Box

east to west. The birds prefer heavy cover for shelter, but require open areas to hunt for small rodents, so that is where Billy built his boxes. They are mounted ten to fifteen feet up an appropriate tree in the deep forest.

Billy said he had six boxes to check. After the first five, we had not seen an owl. The technique is to sneak up to the tree and then tap a few times on the trunk. If the bird is there, it will invariably stick its head out of the hole to assess the disturbance. If an owl is found, Billy will contact his colleague from Antigonish, Dr. Randy Lauf, who studies owls in Nova Scotia. Dr. Lauf will come, open the hinged box, band the owl and its offspring, if any, and record the data. The box is checked at intervals to determine the outcome of breeding.

Upon arrival at box number six, the most difficult to find and approach, we tapped and, sure enough, the little raptor peeked out at us. I got a couple of quick cellphone pics, then we departed quickly to avoid disturbing the bird. This was a great thrill for me. I did not attend the next visit, but two young were found and banded. In birding etiquette, it is permissible to list an owl if you have identified it by sound, but it is much more satisfying to see one. Before long, I had seen several barred owls, much larger and louder than the diminutive Saw-whet.

My next birding adventure was a search for the American Woodcock, a shorebird by genetics but a forest bird by behavior. Seldom seen except by accident, this bird looks like a ball of mud impaled on a stick. It begins its breeding in late winter by flying into the air and making very strange buzzing sounds, after which it drops precipitously to the ground.

 *I probably attempted something similar while in college to attract a mate, with no success.*

The Woodcock typically begins its ritual just after sunset or just before sunrise, times that are dark and cold. Once breeding takes place, the flights are replaced by a persistent *peent* call that lasts all night. Father George MacInnis, another birder I befriended, claims the woodcocks on his property keep him awake all night from early March until mid-April. I had never seen a Woodcock, or couldn't remember where I had seen one, so I inquired and got recommendations to find an open and damp area adjacent to the forest.

I finally found such a place, a hayfield bordered by forest near McNabs Cove. I went in the evening and was very cold and ready to leave when I heard the distinctive call. I had missed the period of skyrocketing. I looked everywhere but could not spook or spot a bird. I returned on several occasions until finally, a Woodcock flew across the open field in front of me to get back to cover. This was my first life bird in Nova Scotia. I made a plan to start earlier and get better looks the following winter. In retrospect, this was life bird 771 and the first of a succession of life birds that would get me close to a landmark achievement.

Next, it was spring, and the Wood-Warblers were the subject of interest—they are elusive, spectacular to see and hear, and only conspicuous for a few weeks. I went out with Billy and his friend Weldon MacPhail, a carpenter and serious carver of ducks, in search of the Canada Warbler. It nests predominantly in Canada and has been in rapid decline. It prefers to be in low foliage, where, once found, it is relatively easy to observe. In contrast, many of its warbler cousins prefer the forest canopy, and the search for them can cause an unpleasant affliction known to birders as "warbler neck."

We went very early to Mill Pond—only one or two kilometers from St. Peter's, but well- hidden unless you know where to look. The pond is named after a grist mill that was once powered by the brook that feeds the pond. The path into the pond is dense and wet, but full of various colorful frog species and some carnivorous plants. The woods were cacophonous with warbler songs, but our goal was to scour the edge of the pond where my friends had seen Canada Warblers in previous years.

We got to our spot and saw many interesting birds, but no Canada Warbler. Two more trips were also unsuccessful. I returned once by myself but got lost. I had not paid enough attention to the trail when I was guided and had forgotten to scatter breadcrumbs. This area is rich in carnivorous pitcher plants and the orchid called Lady's Slipper, so the effort was a success despite missing the Canada Warbler.

Soon thereafter, I bumped into Tyler at a walk to Point Michaud, organized by Professor David McCorquodale, a biologist at Cape Breton University. Tyler and I had met on a previous trip to Cape Breton. He sold us some furniture, and when I asked if he knew any local birders, he confessed to being a birder and photographer himself. Before returning to Cape Breton, I sent him several of my bird guides, which I had hoarded in Colorado and no longer needed. I also told him about my frustrating attempts to find a Canada Warbler.

Tyler is a true "Caper," born and raised in Cape Breton. He seldom ventures more than 20 kilometers from Sydney Municipality, where he lives. He told me he had found a cooperative Canada Warbler in Sydney River, about 60 kilometers east of McNabs Cove. I joined him for a day of birding during which we found a demonstrative Canada Warbler, my first. The bird was located in a cul-de-sac near Sydney River. He appeared immediately in response to Tyler's recorded call and landed in a low bush where I could see the dramatic black necklace traversing its bright yellow breast. It had a grey cap and a white ring around the eyes. This was life bird 772. We made a hasty departure to another location to avoid disturbing the bird anymore.

Tyler had a recording that he called "the mob call," which consists of a hooting Screech Owl accompanied by other birds, such as Black-capped Chickadees, giving alarm calls in response to the owl. Tyler put the recorder on the roof of the car and let it repeat indefinitely. Within one or two minutes, dozens of birds materialized from the forest, obviously alarmed, and in the open where we could view them. This was fun and exciting, but seemed incongruous with our hasty retreat from the Canada warbler.

Many birders take exception to this technique, which is reputed to be used more often by bird photographers than purist birders, to allow a better chance to get a good photograph. There is no question that it works and creates an exciting experience. The ethics of this approach are certainly questionable, but Tyler uses it selectively and is concerned about disturbing nesting birds. Once he has photographed a bird, he minimizes returning to that site to make sure the bird is not

Canada Warbler

Canada Warbler
Photograph Provided by Steven McGrath

overstressed. He is also very secretive about his bird observations; I was lucky to be trusted enough to join him on that very special day.

During my day with Tyler, I told him I was keen to see a Veery, a thrush that typically lurks in nearly impenetrable wet habitats of thick growth and insects. I had never seen one. As we were driving along a dirt road, we thought we saw one fly from the road into the forest, but we were unable to tease it out to get a look. About a week later, Tyler called to tell me that he had found a Veery occupying the same hedge where he had observed and photographed a Chestnut-sided Warbler, also uncommon in Cape Breton. The Veery had been there long enough to recognize the call of the warbler, and, remarkably, responded to it as if the two were conversing.

The next day, I met Tyler after he got off work, and we sought and found the bird, a nearly orange thrush with the call veeery from which it got its name. Tyler was able to get a diagnostic photograph, which started me thinking again that it was time for me to take up photography. My thanks and kudos to Tyler for finding the Veery for me and taking the time to show me. I haven't seen much of him since he went back to work after a COVID interruption, but he is the type of friend who you know is there when you need him, common among birders, who tend to be loners. Typical of a Cape Bretoner, or Caper, he calls me "Buddy." The Veery, a thrush, was life bird 773.

Let's go next to Point Michaud. It is a prime spot in North America for Nelson's Sparrow, previously the Sharp-tailed Sparrow, but subsequently split into Nelson's and Saltmarsh Sparrows. I had heard the bird twice without a glimpse, in Minnesota and North

Veery

Veery
Photograph Provided by Tyler Day

Dakota, and had seen it in Texas, where it was silent. Point Michaud, not more than 15 minutes from McNabs Cove, juts out into the Gulf of Maine with pebbly sand beaches on both sides of a trail that meanders between both shores. The sparrows prefer the grass that grows along the dunes.

I was with a small group of Cape Breton birders on a walk organized by David McCorquodale. It was early summer, 2021. We walked along the coast toward the Point and soon heard the unique sound—not a song, more a call or a rattle—like water dropped on a heated skillet. It took a bit longer to get a good look, but the bird eventually had the decency to pop up briefly to perch on the high grass and assess the situation. We got good but brief looks, and the photographers got good photographs. We could see the orange face framed by a dark cap and a white throat. This was the first meaningful and complete experience with this bird for me, despite several close calls, which gave it a hallowed spot on my Life List, life bird number 774.

Finally, I come to the first rare and truly miraculous bird I saw in Nova Scotia, but it was not in Cape Breton. The bird was a Grey Heron, found near the Bay of Fundy in western Nova Scotia. It was being seen regularly—but not daily—in Miner's Marsh, a small and elegant park owned by Ducks Unlimited in the town of Kentville. The park is used by locals as a place to walk and get close to nature. After monitoring the bird's behavior and typical times of its sightings, I decided to time the five-hour drive to arrive mid-afternoon, stay overnight to allow a second chance, if necessary, and return home. Aura and I arrived at the appointed time, and I spotted the expected group of birders with scopes and cameras. Unfortunately,

Nelson's Sparrow - Photograph
by Steven McGrath

Grey Heron - Photograph Provided
by Rowland Spears

they were talking and not looking at anything; it was obvious the bird wasn't there.

Although the Grey Heron did not appear that day, I was delighted to spot it the following morning. It was perched on a magnifi cent old hemlock tree that displayed a striking dead snag. I was accompanied by Rowland Spears, a talented bird photographer who appreciated the view as much as I did. He already had taken photographs that he was kind enough to share. This was the first Grey Heron ever seen in Nova Scotia. It is a European heron, similar to our common Great Blue Heron. Another Grey Heron, perhaps the same bird, appeared near Yarmouth the next winter.

Why he was in Nova Scotia is an unanswerable question, since birds don't give interviews or provide itineraries, but who cares? He was there, and so was I. The heron was another life bird, my fourth since my arrival in Cape Breton in March 2020. I decided to update my ABA checklist of North American birds, which constantly changes as species are lumped or split, and determine how many birds I had on my life list.

The counting process is akin to a root canal, but necessary from time to time if you are a bird lister.

The Grey Heron gave me 775 birds, enough to put me in the rarified atmosphere of some 200 birders, give or take a few, who have listed more than 700 birds in the American Birding Association's version of North America.

I was excited but humbled by this finding, and began to allow myself to think about the goal of 800 life birds. I did some research and found, to my amazement, that there were only 56 birders who were willing to admit that they had seen 800 species. At age 75, I wouldn't have much time, but newly retired, I might have a chance.

A couple of months later, in autumn 2020, another rare heron showed up in Pictou, Nova Scotia, near the mooring of the Prince Edward Island ferry on Caribou Island. This was a Little Egret, a bird that is common in Africa and parts of Europe but accidental along the northeastern coast of North America. One had been present near Portland, Maine, the previous year, but I couldn't go after it because the border was closed. The bird in Pictou was reported on a Saturday, and my friend Tyler Day was nice enough to inform me. The location of the sighting was about a two-hour drive, so I decided to go for it the next morning.

I set out and called Tyler, who was monitoring the bird. He told me that it hadn't been seen yet that day. I continued and arrived uneventfully at the site, where other birders, including the ubiquitous Rowland Spears, were already present. No one had seen the bird. I stayed for several hours but had to leave by 3:30 p.m. to get home in time for my weekly Zoom with my children. The Little Egret was seen briefly the next morning, and then it vanished. This is a common theme among birders that I have experienced all too often: a near miss, much worse than being days late. I always go back for more punishment and, more often than not, find the bird I'm looking for.

Two days later, I noticed a posting on the Nova Scotia bird website that someone had seen the bird at 4:30 p.m., one hour after my departure. But I was later informed that this report came from someone who had the unfortunate reputation of making inaccurate reports of bird sightings. Yes, even birders cheat or, to be kind, can turn delusions into reality. Perhaps that is one reason why we seek birds; they don't cheat and are seldom delusional.

About four weeks later, another or perhaps the same Little Egret turned up near Sydney, Nova Scotia at Dominion Beach Park. I rushed there the next day and found the bird immediately. I called Steve McGrath, who had seen and reported the bird the day before,

Little Egret - Photograph Provided by Steven McGrath

Note the small plume on the neck, the grey-blue bill extending to the eye, and the greenish-yellow legs.

and thanked him for his kind directions to the spot. I had the bird in view in my spotting scope as I spoke, lifer number 776.

Another week later, as I had hoped and expected, a Barnacle Goose was reported in Shaw's Pond near the town of Truro, again about a two-hour drive from my home. This rare goose, which nests in Greenland, is seen nearly every year in Nova Scotia, but does not linger.

I missed one that was present for one day in Colorado two years prior.

Barnacle Goose with Canada Geese
Cellphone Photograph

Barnacle Goose - Photograph Provided
by Steven McGrath

The bird was not reported again for a few days, so I waited. On Saturday at about noon, I saw a report that the goose had been seen that morning. Within 15 minutes, I had packed a lunch and my gear and was on my way to Shaw's Pond.

As I drove, I contacted Steve McGrath to see if he knew anyone who might be at the pond and who would know if the goose was there. Steve contacted Ron Dane, a respected birder from Halifax. Ron told Steve the goose was best seen in the early morning or in the evening when it returned to the pond from grazing in nearby cultivated fields. I planned to arrive about 4 p.m., look for the goose, and stay overnight to bird with Ron the next morning, if necessary.

Upon arrival, I observed scores of First Nation people from the Millbrook Reserve fishing in the river near my destination. They were catching striped bass, which run in abundance this time of year in some rivers. I scanned the hundreds of Canada Geese on the pond, failed to find the Barnacle goose, and then took a short ride along the road to search for grazing geese before returning to Shaw's Pond. A flock of geese flew in and landed as I approached. I went to another spot to scan the pond from a different angle, and, within a few minutes, moved my glasses from several Canada Geese to one conspicuously different goose. It was the Barnacle!

"There you are," I heard myself say—a gross understatement considering previous frustrating near-misses.

I studied the bird and identified the striking white face compared to that of the Canada Goose, which has just a patch of white, and its dark breast extending to the water, while the Canada Goose has a dark neck but a light-grey breast. The Barnacle also had a thin black line running from the beak to its eye and a relatively stubby bill. With no question of the identity and nothing more to see, I called Aura, headed for home, and arrived at 7:15 p.m. in time for a good meal and a celebratory beverage.

I had just seen life bird number 777 in North America. I texted a cellphone photo to my kids in which I challenged them, similarly to "Where's Waldo," to identify the Barnacle Goose surrounded by Canada Geese. None was able to find it. The same thing could have happened to me, but it didn't, and I was one coveted and twice-missed bird closer to 800 life birds.

I FIND MY FIRST NORTHERN LAPWING

It was a Friday evening in 2020, and the Jewish Sabbath (Shabbat). Aura and I were relaxing after spending two hours on our new porch, where we conducted our Shabbat rituals and ate our Shabbat meal under the glow and warmth of our propane heater, despite a November temperature of 7°C. I picked up my phone to check the Nova Scotia rare bird reports as I do every evening. The phone had been silenced for the Sabbath. I noticed that I had a call from fellow birder David McCorquodale. I looked at the list of posted birds and noticed, with shock, that a Northern Lapwing had been found that day in a place only a three-hour drive from McNabs Cove.

This was not just another rare bird. I had a history with it.

About eight years before that, in January 2013, I became aware that Northern Lapwings were being reported daily from Newfoundland. I was still living in Denver and had never seen this spectacular bird, which is common in Europe but accidental in North America. It would also be the first time I went to Newfoundland. Aura, a non-birder, is a good sport when it comes to my birding escapades. Always ready for an adventure, she agreed to go. We booked a flight from Denver to Newark with a connection to St. John's, Newfoundland.

Everything went well until we were flying over St. John's through clear skies. We could see the airport below, but we were above broken clouds; it was snowing below. The pilot inexplicably decided not to land, and instead diverted to Deer Lake, Newfoundland, a few hundred miles west, where he could land and, he hoped, get clearance to land in St. John's. It didn't work out that way. The pilot used up his flying time as we shivered and starved on the plane, since there was no Customs in Deer Lake. Ultimately, we had to return to Newark, arriving at 3 a.m. A young man sitting behind us was in tears. He had traveled from Scotland for a weekend with his girlfriend, and now his time was cut in half or worse.

Nothing was open, not even Starbucks. A McDonald's opened at about 6 a.m. We gulped down a breakfast sandwich and bought one

Tufted Duck

Black-Tailed Gull

Dovekies

Dovekie - Photograph Taken by
Me in the St. Peter's Canal, N .S.

for our distraught Scot. We then booked a flight to Toronto, which departed at 9 a.m., finally making it to St. John's in the early evening, thirty-six grueling hours after we departed from Denver. There was fresh snow on the ground, but nothing else seemed amiss.

Early the next morning, we set out with our guide, Dave Brown, to find the Lapwings and other target birds. One of those was the Tufted Duck, which I had missed on several previous attempts. Dave expressed concern that the storm might have affected the Lapwings. He was right, they were gone.

Aside from the Lapwing disaster, we enjoyed our first time in Newfoundland. I saw my first Tufted Duck. I also saw my first Dovekie, a tiny seabird of northern latitudes, and my first Black-tailed Gull, a very rare bird for North America, which we found easily at the famous birding spot, Quidi Vidi Lake in St. John's. We enjoyed the

Palette abstract of Newfoundland birds

music and pubs on George St. and got "screeched in," the ritual by which visitors become official Newfies by drinking rum and kissing a codfish in an overcrowded bar. At Aura's suggestion, we picked up the dinner tab for a solo American soldier whom we learned was awaiting military transport home after many months of duty in Iraq. His smile made our day.

A couple of years later, there was a report of a Northern Lapwing wintering on Nantucket Island. We needed to wait until April to look for it so we could meet my daughter and family, as usual, in nearby Martha's Vineyard for our annual spring break reunion. When we arrived at our bed and breakfast in Nantucket, I checked the North American Rare Bird Alert and discovered, sadly, that the bird, present when we left Denver, had not been seen that day. It was indeed missing the next day as well and every day thereafter. We had missed it again.

So, here it was again, a Northern Lapwing, this time in Cape Breton. I would look for it, of course, but without optimism. Steve McGrath picked me up at 7:30 a.m. I had not slept well. We headed for Port Hawkesbury, where we met David McCorquodale and switched cars. We set out for the remote fishing village of Canso to look for the Lapwing. None of us had ever seen one in North America, although David had seen one in the UK, where it is common. We got a text from Mark Dennis that he had seen the bird before it flew away. I said to myself: "Here we go again."

When we arrived at the site, a soccer field, the bird was still absent, but Dr. Ken McKenna had arrived from his home near Pictou, a village in Northumberland on the Nova Scotia mainland. This was a good omen, as he is a superb birder. We assessed the area, and the group

Canso Graveyard　　　　　　　Lapwing-less soccer field

decided that I should be posted in a graveyard on a hill overlooking the fields where the Lapwing had been spotted. The others would scout around. I would text if the bird came in.

I asked David, facetiously: "Should I take it personally that you're dumping me in a graveyard, and is there any risk you won't come back? It's a long walk back to Cape Breton from Canso." He chuckled but said nothing. As I entered the ancient graveyard, I had a flashback to a traumatic episode that occurred when I was a toddler in a Dickensian nursery school in Ohio. It was winter, and I had so much difficulty getting into my winter gear, including leggings, that I missed recess and was humiliated by being told to go out and play by myself. Nevertheless, I was willing to accept the discomfort that came with the opportunity to be the first to spot the Lapwing.

The graveyard is the highest point in town and has a perfect view of the habitat where we hoped to see the bird. There were a few people there digging a grave and curious about what I was doing prowling around the graveyard with binoculars. The sighting of ghosts, to the best of my knowledge, does not require binoculars.

"What's up?" the woman gravedigger asked.

"We're here from Cape Breton looking for a rare bird that was seen this morning down on the soccer field," I replied.

I showed them a photo of a Lapwing. This was my first birding experience with gravediggers, but they seemed genuinely interested. While I was there, I visited several ancient graves covered with orange lichen, with some of the graves dating back to the early 19th century. There was a huge crucifix on which roosted a few vigilant ravens. I expected one to say, "Nevermore." There were a few small birds of interest, but after two hours with the spirits, no Lapwing.

My fellow birders did come back for me, and we decided to check out some areas for other birds, then return and look for the Lapwing again. In the process, we got cold and wet as the weather deteriorated. When we returned to the fields, the bird was still absent. We decided to give up, but Ken suggested checking the soccer field at the local school, Hazel Hill, which he had identified on Google Earth as a grassy open area, the preferred habitat for a Lapwing. We agreed to do it, but our heads were hanging in frustration. It took a while to locate the school, which we would never have found without our GPS. As we approached the parking lot, I spotted a flock of Canada Geese. I scanned the birds carefully, looking for a Barnacle Goose or some other rarity.

Seeing nothing unusual, my eyes drifted right to the grassy sports field. I noticed something moving. After a few seconds of shocked silence, I yelled out, "That's it—there's the Lapwing!"

Everyone shouted "Where?" and I replied, "Right in the middle of the bleeping field!"

They all spotted the bird. We tried to dampen our celebration to avoid spooking our bird as photos were snapped and until Ken, who hadn't yet arrived, had been texted and was able to join us. I got the bird in my scope and studied it.

Was this real, or a birder's hallucination?

This was no ordinary bird. A member of the plover family of shorebirds, it had a greenish back, a black collar on its breast, distinct black linear marks on the face, and a small plume that extended backward from the head. When it flew, which it did several times while we watched, it emitted an alarming screech, after which it extended its relatively long wings, the underside of which had a striking black-and-white pattern. It hovered before descending to the ground, as if attached to a parachute. I have never seen any bird act this way. As we watched, it put on a show that we could never have anticipated, then flew away as the photographers crept closer to get better photos. This was a bird worth "watching," despite my objection to the derogatory term, bird watcher.

At least four of us had never seen this bird. We gave each other high elbows (COVID behavior) and allowed ourselves to celebrate a bit and take photos of one another and the school sign. I congratulated Ken on his wise recommendation to check the school and told him that I was no longer a jinx, something he had suggested earlier, presumably

My Northern Lapwing - Photograph
Provided by Rowland Spears

Northern Lapwing

in jest. I returned, shivering, to McNabs Cove after phoning Aura to share the good news. She understood—she had been there with me for both previous failures.

I walked into the house wet and cold, but as happy as an inveterate birder can be, into the warmth of our Canadian home, *Unama'kik*, and the company of my wife, who had a homemade pizza in the oven.

Unama'kik is the indigenous word for Cape Breton, which loosely translates to land of fog.

Several hours later, the whole saga still felt surreal, but the posted reports confirmed that it happened. I had seen North American bird number 778, perhaps the best one of all thus far.

Steller's Sea Eagle

Common Shelduck - Life Bird 779

A LOST EAGLE BREAKS MY HEART
AND WE RETURN TO COLORADO

RULE 30
You can't go home again.

I t was a Thursday night at bedtime, late autumn in 2021, and all was calm. I opened my tablet to do a little reading and check the news, my customary bedtime routine. When I checked the Nova Scotia Rare Bird alert, I was shocked to discover that an extraordinarily rare bird, never before seen in Nova Scotia, had been discovered about a three-hour drive away in the town of Windsor. It was a Steller's Sea Eagle, a gigantic raptor that is normally found on the Kamchatka Peninsula of Siberia and northeast coastal Asia. It had been seen sporadically during that summer in various parts of the Gaspé Peninsula in Quebec. A few Nova Scotia birders made the 10-hour drive to Gaspé with no luck. Undoubtedly, this was the same bird.

A gang of birders had posted that they had seen the bird. This group included many of the *who's who* of Nova Scotia birders, and I was not one of them. The group included Ken McKenna, with whom I had shared my room for our pelagic trip in Pubnico the preceding August. I'm certain that he and the others were so excited and anxious to get to the site that they simply forgot about everybody else. I wasn't a member of the club. At first, I took this personally, but I realized eventually that this was a cultural norm in Nova Scotia; I would have to earn my way into the community of birders over time. I was, and still am, averse to social media; I hadn't adapted to modern behavior and paid the price.

I decided, based on the erratic behavior of the bird, to wait for a report indicating that it was still present before making the seven-hour round-trip drive. I was already exhausted from a stressful trip to Halifax a few days before for Aura's immigration physical. I fell asleep and missed an email message from David McCorquodale, asking me if I planned to go after the bird. In the morning, I texted Ken, who said that he believed the bird was still there and that he would keep me posted. David was already on his way there from Cape Breton. Within minutes, I was on my way, with an ETA of about 2:30 p.m.

As I passed Antigonish, nearly halfway, Ken texted that David had seen the bird. My pulse must have been 200; this was a once-in-a-lifetime chance to find this bird in North America, or so I thought. About an hour later, Ken reported that the eagle had flown out of sight and hadn't been seen since, but I had passed the point of no return and continued to the destination, where a crowd of disappointed birders looked dazed but hopeful. I searched the rest of the day until darkness, without seeing the eagle, found a motel, and returned to the site at daybreak; no eagle. I finally gave up and returned to Cape Breton and my sympathetic wife with a hangdog face I couldn't conceal.

Of all my birding experiences over decades, I had never been so disappointed. I couldn't help feeling a sense of betrayal by several fellow birders whose companionship I had sought and for whom I had provided hospitality of one form or another. On the other hand, I could have arrived earlier if I hadn't been so cautious (and exhausted), and then I would have seen the eagle—my choice not to take the "road less traveled." If I had seen and responded to David's email, he would have told me that he planned to leave before dark to arrive as early as possible. Finally, I hadn't put in the time and effort to earn my membership among the elite birders. Still, I had a premonition that I would have another opportunity to see this conspicuous and rare bird—and I was right.

Early in 2022, the North American Rare Bird Alert reported that a Steller's Sea Eagle had been found in the vicinity of Bristol in Southern Massachusetts. It was believed to be the same bird that had been seen in both the Gaspé Peninsula and Nova Scotia because of its extreme rarity, so far from its normal habitat. My daughter Jennifer lives about 45 minutes from Bristol in Manomet, Massachusetts. I called her and told her the whole sad story. She said she had some time and would drive to Bristol to look for the bird. If she could, she would share it with me on FaceTime so that I could experience the bird in real time. I decided that, if we could pull this off, I would put the bird on my list even though, strictly speaking, it would not be "countable." Unfortunately, when I checked on the eagle's status, I found that it had disappeared.

A few weeks later, the eagle was found around Boothbay Harbor, Maine. This is an area of points of land protruding into the ocean so that there are countless places where the bird could hide, or be seen. There were numerous sightings over the next few weeks, including just days before our planned return to Colorado, where I would get some much-needed medical care for refractory asthma, and sell our downtown loft. We would pass through Maine, Massachusetts, and New Jersey before heading west to Denver.

Then, predictably, the eagle disappeared. About two weeks later, on Valentine's Day, it was re-found about 30 minutes from Boothbay Harbor, at a bridge that goes to the town of Arrowsic across the Black River. We had already booked lodging in Boothbay Harbor, so we planned to search for the bird, but our time would be limited. The proprietor of our inn arranged for me to be invited to join a Steller's Sea Eagle group online from which I could get constant reports of the bird's status.

As we approached the area, it became clear that dozens of birders were out in various locations with no credible sightings. It appeared to me that some sort of post-COVID group hysteria had developed over this rare bird, which was drawing not just birders, but others seeking an adventure. I learned that Wellington Biggins, who had led my trip to the Dry Tortugas, was on his way from Florida to look for the eagle.

We chose the circuitous coastal route into Boothbay Harbor to be closer to any reported sightings. We arrived exhausted after a 10-hour drive. We didn't spot the bird, nor were there any reported sightings that day, but we planned to visit the bridge where it had been spotted. After sleeping about 12 hours, we had breakfast and set out on our voyage. As we arrived late in the morning at the bridge, I immediately spotted Wellington.

"Hey Welly," I said, as we pulled our truck close to where he was standing on the bridge with his binoculars. He responded but didn't recognize me until I told him my name. It had been at least 20 years since I last saw him.

In true form, he looked at Aura and asked me, "How did you manage to marry such a beautiful woman?"

I replied, "I guess I'm pretty attractive as birders go."

We parked the truck, and I cruised through the group of birders to get an update. I was told there had not been any sightings that day, but there was no doubt the bird had been seen there several times just days earlier. Unfortunately, I was not in a position to linger for hours or days in the area, and we decided to continue our trip. Moreover, a circus-like atmosphere had developed, which included lots of idle chatter online. Locals were becoming hostile toward the swarms of birders who parked along the narrow roads and often drove erratically. As I stood on the bridge, I heard honking and obscenities from the good people of coastal Maine as they drove past. Unfortunately, they had good reason.

I had some more optimistic thoughts. Perhaps the unprecedented obsession of so many to see this magnificent bird was a good thing. If they were searching for beauty and adventure, they qualified as true birders and might eventually acquire the knowledge and skills to be successful. Hopefully, they will continue their new interest beyond the Steller's Sea Eagle.

There were no sightings that day. After a four-hour trip, we arrived in Sandwich, Massachusetts, and had a wonderful visit with my daughter Jennifer, her husband Dave, and my two grandchildren, Annie and Ben. I got to meet Annie's boyfriend, Hugo, and his parents. Annie and Hugo are performers and had just returned from auditioning for the play *Chicago*. We returned to our lodging, the charming Belfry Inn and Bistro in Sandwich, where we endured a wild night of gale-force winds that shook the old converted church to its foundation.

After breakfast the next morning, I checked the eagle hotline and was stunned to see that a fly-by had been spotted. Soon thereafter, the bird, nicknamed Stella, was perched in a tree and photographed just yards from where we had stood 24 hours earlier. I had missed it again. This time, I was much more philosophical about the disappointment. Seeing a majestic, rare bird in the company of hundreds of crazed birders was not the experience I sought. I had seen so many photos of this eagle and visited places where it had been that it seemed as though it wouldn't make much difference to see it in the flesh. This bird, along with eagles in general, had taken on a mystical significance for me that transcended the usual issues I consider in birding. I might compare it, for example, to the mythical white whale in *Moby Dick*—maybe I was better off having a good story to explain the emptiest spot on my life list of birds.

I am certain I have grown from this painful experience, but I cannot conceal or deny my vulnerability to personal failure which has always been the source of my overachieving behavior. In this context, the elusive eagle became my teacher in absentia, a harbinger of insights more likely to be learned in the autumn of life, and my motivation for continuing my quest.

After our brief visit with Jen and her family, we drove to Wyckoff, New Jersey to see our daughter Leah and her husband Tyler. Leah was quite pregnant and getting close to delivery. She was happy to see us, but very uncomfortable. We didn't stay long, and we knew that Aura would be summoned back as soon as the baby was born. From Wyckoff, it took us two long days to get to Denver, where we would get our loft ready to sell and where I would get some medical attention for my worsening respiratory condition. Back to reality.

On the way to Denver, we passed through southern Pennsylvania, where many Amish people live. A Common Shelduck (life bird 779)—normally found in northern Europe and Siberia—had been reported on a rural pond. We meandered around a bit and finally found the pond, where I also found the bird. It was a life bird and provided some consolation for missing the eagle.

As we were in Denver doing what had to be done, I had the opportunity to spend some time with my daughter Patty, who is an ophthalmology research technologist. We also saw our best friends, Jonathan and Leslie Levy, who had moved to Denver a few years before from New York City, now just a short drive from Leah's house in Wyckoff.

Despite several positive experiences in Denver, we sensed that something had changed, and not for the better. After four years of political division and two years of the pandemic, there was a tangible atmosphere of angst and anger everywhere we went. We saw it on the streets of Denver amid countless closed shops and restaurants. We saw it on the highways, where people drove with a flagrant lack of courtesy, and in our building, where we were falsely accused of putting a dent in a renter's car and tampering with the mail of the new occupants of our former loft.

It was clear that it had become unwise to discuss politics or social issues with anyone unless you were already aware that they shared your views. In short, it wasn't the same place we had left so precipitously three years earlier. We had made the right decision to sell the loft where we had once enjoyed urban life.

This was the experience that Thomas Wolfe wrote about in his book, You Can't Go Home Again, published posthumously. The book is an autobiographical account of leaving Asheville, North Carolina, and returning there after living in New York and traveling the world. He and his world views had changed, and he no longer fit in.

To us, it wasn't just a matter of the city; the entire United States of America—post-January 6, 2021—seemed hopelessly divided and no longer felt like home. Thus far, nothing has happened to change this reality.

Not long after arriving in Denver, Aura's first grandchild, Hudson Allen Pitman, was born. Leah was quite ill after the delivery, and Aura rushed to New Jersey, where she provided sorely needed respite. I remained in Denver and continued my various doctors' appointments and tests while downsizing our possessions. Within a few weeks, our loft was sold, and we were expatriates.

RULE 31
One rare bird found is worth at least two missed.

In 2023, we were back in Cape Breton, and I learned that there were at least three lifers being seen regularly in south Texas. The guide I booked, Tiffany Kersten, set the world record in 2021 for a "Big Year," the most birds seen in one year in the lower 48 states. I didn't know this when I booked her. Ironically, she set the record by seeing 778 birds, similar to the number that I had seen in my five decades of persistent, opportunistic birding.

I planned to stay at the Alamo Inn, where I had always stayed on previous trips to the area. The Inn caters to birders, is strategically situated, and offers self-serve coffee and breakfast as early as is necessary to get after the birds. My room, shown below, was tiny but had everything I needed. It reminded me of a famous painting by iconic artist Van Gogh, "Bedroom in Arles."

My trip from Denver to McAllen, Texas was pleasant. It was my first time flying since the beginning of the pandemic. People were well-behaved, despite reports on other flights of unruly passengers who resented the appropriate COVID precautions. Some had developed tricks to avoid masking, such as having a series of beverages so that they could have their masks off as they sipped incessantly.

I expected Tiffany at 6 a.m. and was in my car and ready to go at the appointed time. We would use separate cars to avoid exposure—a wise choice, I thought. However, there was a misunderstanding about our meeting location, so Tiffany was waiting for me seven miles away at the bat falcon site. I called and managed to find her, but she hadn't seen the bird. We checked its other preferred location with no luck. As we searched, I noticed that Tiffany used only a spotting scope when guiding, no binoculars or cameras. Once she had found the bird, I understood, this would allow her to show it to her clients, who would likely be less skillful. She was keen to please her troops.

Undismayed, we drove to Brownsville to look for the Social Flycatcher. The weather was unfavorable, foggy and cold, and we couldn't find the Social Flycatcher. We did, however, see flocks of Red-crowned Parrots and Green Parakeets, countable birds if seen

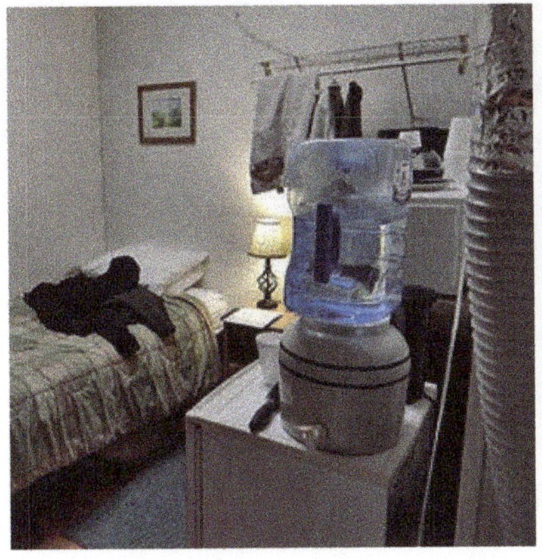

My Alamo, Texas Version of
Van Gogh's Room

Red-Crowned Parrot - Painting by Peggy
Rowlett After Photograph by Author

in Texas, but already on my list, seen in Florida. I managed to get a spectacular photo of one of the parrots, which has now become a painting done by my Denver neighbor, Peggy Rowlett.

We left the Social Flycatcher site with some frustration and anxiety to find the Golden-crowned Warbler in Weslaco. There, we found a quiet place where I was fascinated by Tiffany's approach to finding the tiny bird. She walked silently and discouraged any conversation as she listened for the clicking notes of the diminutive warbler, which was not breeding and, therefore, not singing. We walked the trails until she stopped and pointed to where she heard the sound. I heard nothing. "That's it," she said, with conviction.

I trained my glasses on a lush area of foliage near the ground where the warbler skulked. Finally, it popped into the open, and I got a good look at its yellow breast and olive-green back. I saw the striped crown that, to me, was more white than golden.

Crown (cap): That part of a bird from which a tuft extends if the bird has a tuft or where the bird sports a kippah if Jewish, a sombrero if Mexican, or a beanie if pledged to a fraternity.

I switched to my camera and took dozens of exposures, only one of which captured the bird. But that was more than enough. I had the proof and had seen life bird number 780. This rare warbler was

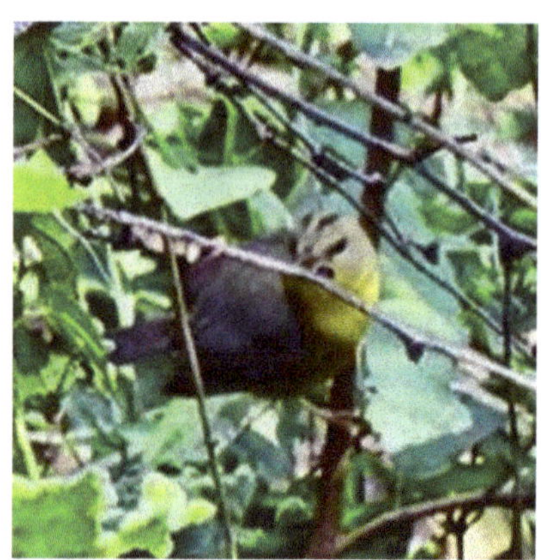

Golden-crowned Warbler

the first lifer of the trip and broke the proverbial ice. I could relax, at least a bit.

We traveled next to the Laguna Atascosa Refuge, where Aplomado Falcons were nesting. These handsome raptors had once patrolled the open areas of the lower Rio Grande Valley and southeastern Arizona but had not been recorded in those areas since the 1930s. A re-population effort in Texas has been successful, and the bird is now countable, though restricted in its territory.

Once we had driven into the refuge and gotten out of our cars, Tiffany scanned the terrain and said, to my shock, "I think I have the bird over there on the nesting post." The post consisted of a platform and a post in the middle of an open field serenaded by singing Western Meadowlarks. The platform had been provided by the refuge to encourage nesting.

The Aplomado Falcon was barely visible on the far side of the platform, but I could make out its characteristic facial "moustache." I attempted to photograph it but got only enough for identification. While it wasn't the view I'd hoped for, this was still a life bird, number 781, a bird brought back from the brink of extinction and a species I had never expected to see. As such, it joined the company on my list with the California Condor, Whooping Crane, Peregrine Falcon, and Kirtland's Warbler, all of which were saved by the efforts of those who cared enough to muster the necessary resources and scientific information. This was not just a day of life birds but one of appreciation for those whose hard work and love of Planet Earth saved a beautiful bird and made my sighting possible.

Aplomado Falcon on the Nesting
Platform - Note the Dark Head
Contrasted with the Lighter Underparts

Aplomado Falcon
life bird 781

It was getting late, so we made a plan for the next day. We would meet at Bentsen State Park to look for the Hook-billed Kite and then return to Brownsville for the Social Flycatcher, which had been seen after we left. The weather was going to clear by afternoon and get warmer, which would improve our chances.

It was time for a solo run to Santa Ana to look for the Bat Falcon. I found many birders there, along with terrible traffic and noise. I stayed until dark, with no luck. Several additional trips would also yield nothing other than a few Kestrels, which flew in from a distance and caused some excitement before they were close enough to be identified. The Bat Falcon was not seen again. One down, but nothing new in my birding saga.

The next morning, I met Tiffany at Bentsen State Park. We walked out to the observation deck early in the morning, where we found the area shrouded in dense fog, not conducive to finding Hook-billed Kites. Still, we were dazzled by several Vermilion Flycatchers, arguably the most handsome of this family of birds. We didn't stay long and headed back to Brownsville for an all-out effort to find the Social Flycatcher, hoping to benefit from clear skies and warming temperatures.

In Brownsville, we scouted all the usual sites where the bird had been seen. The favored area was from a bridge that was a major route for students crossing the sprawling campus.. The dominant bird was the Great Kiskadee, a flycatcher that resembles the Social Flycatcher, but is larger, raucous, and has a huge bill. We were on the

Social Flycatcher

Social Flycatcher Socializing
with Hooded Oriole

lookout for the less common Tropical Kingbirds, because we were more likely to find the Social Flycatcher in their company for reasons that were unclear to us, but which I'm sure the Social Flycatcher would explain if it could.

After a couple of hours of increasing anxiety and many Kiskadees, which I tried unsuccessfully to make into the Social Flycatcher, a Tropical Kingbird arrived. It was early afternoon, and as predicted, the sky had cleared and the temperature had become seasonably warm. The Tropical Kingbird was solo and perched in a tree in an open area of grass. We raised our alertness and began to search the nooks and crannies. I was assigned to cover the most frequent site on the bridge while Tiffany roamed. I saw her suddenly freeze and point. A bird flew over the road at the end of the bridge and disappeared. We ran to the road and scanned.

Then Tiffany announced, "That's our bird."

The Social Flycatcher reappeared, flew toward us, and landed in a conspicuous open area in its preferred foliage beside the bridge. I got my glasses on the bird, which at first glance looked like a miniature Kiskadee. It was a predominantly yellow bird with a dark grey-brown back and a conspicuous black mask that covers the entire head except for a light crown. But the bill was a tiny stub compared to the sword of the Kiskadee, and our bird had tufts of feathers extending outward from the base of the neck and the characteristic whiskers worn by many flycatchers.

Tiffany "Big Year" Kersten

Vermilion Flycatcher

Whiskers: hairlike feathers that project from the base of the bill and are used to detect edible insects and avoid inedible things like fingers.

Our Social Flycatcher serenaded us with its humble call of two or three sharp notes. Typical of its sociality, it was joined briefly by a Hooded Oriole on its roost, so I was able to photograph both birds in the same field. The Social Flycatcher was life bird 782 and a very rare one at that!

With Tiffany's skill and perseverance, we had found our bird—the first Social Flycatcher reported in North America. (A year later, after a brief disappearance, this charming bird was still being seen at the same location, where it is now projected to receive an honorary degree from the University of Texas.) Tiffany and I walked back to our vehicles triumphantly. Our time together was over, but I had decided to extend my stay to spend more time looking for Hook-billed Kite, and just in case the Bat Falcon was still around. Before we went our separate ways, I asked Tiffany where she had found a Manx Shearwater during her Big Year. She told me that she had found them at Revere Beach in Massachusetts.

A BELATED RETURN TO ARIZONA
AND REUNION WITH MELODY KEHL,
LIFE BIRDS 783 AND 784

Aside from the missed Bat Falcon, it had been a bountiful trip to Texas' Rio Grande Valley. Tiffany "Big Year" Kersten had helped me add four life birds to bring my list to 782, including the rare and captivatingly social, Social Flycatcher. After returning to Denver, I contacted my friend and trusted guide Melody Kehl in Tucson to see if there was anything there worth chasing. I also wanted her to know that I was in Denver and poised to jump at any opportunity. She mentioned the discovery the day before of a Nutting's Flycatcher, which appears yearly, more or less, in Arizona, but usually in the Colorado River area of remote western Arizona, a very difficult place to access. This Nutting's Flycatcher was merely an hour's drive east of Tucson. I told her I would be interested, since it would get me close to seeing every flycatcher on the ABA list. I made plans to go.

I watched the rare bird reports daily as my visit approached. There was one day that the flycatcher was not seen, which created some anxiety. I later found out that Melody was there that day with a client. Undoubtedly, there were too many birders, so the sensible bird would leave its favored area until things were quiet, then return. It was important for us to get there early to avoid this problem. The bird was also being harassed by the resident Ash-throated Flycatchers, which represented an identification challenge since they are so similar to the Nutting's, and also more numerous. The only differences are the lack of a terminal bar on the tail feathers of the Nutting's and a smaller, rounder head. The call, *wheeep*, which the bird utters early and seldom, is diagnostic. When I learned of the absence of my target bird, I considered cancelling the trip, but I knew Melody would let me know if she thought I shouldn't come.

Then I noticed a report of a Ridgway's Rail that was heard by four observers at the Base Meridian Wildlife Area in Maricopa County, west of Phoenix. This bird had been split from the Clapper Rail and is found primarily in salt marshes on the California coast. It would be another life bird for me. None of the observers had seen the bird, but their recordings of its repetitive call were convincing. Although this rail is more common in California, it is still very difficult to see. More reports followed from others who had heard the bird and posted more recordings of its characteristic staccato *kek kek kek* call. I asked Melody for her opinion. She was not enthusiastic. She couldn't go with me and said it would be very difficult to see.

I was intrigued that all the reports were from very early in the morning; none were from the evening, when the birds are also active, according to my research. Finally, the night before my departure, a Utah birder reported hearing the bird in the evening around 7 p.m. An evening sighting would allow me to fly to Tucson, drive to Maricopa, look for the bird, and drive back in time to rest before setting out early the next morning with Melody for the Nutting's Flycatcher. I decided to go for it.

All went as planned, and I arrived at the site about 5 p.m. The location was in a rural area where I noticed a line of roadside stands that offered Mexican food and a variety of paraphernalia as I approached the refuge. When I arrived, I realized that I was parking at a motor speedway that was hosting an event that evening. There were already loud noises of revving cars and raucous music blasting. Surely, all the commotion would prevent the rail from coming out of hiding or even prevent its call. I parked and walked into the refuge, which is situated along the nearly dry Gila River, then followed the coordinates of previous reports on foot to places that seemed appropriate, where there was water and good cover for the skittish rails. I listened, played the call, waited for the sun to set—and heard nothing.

Then, about 7 p.m., I heard a faint call characteristic of the Ridgway's Rail. I walked toward the sound and discovered the Utah birder who had reported hearing the rail the previous evening. He was playing the call, so I had heard his tape, not the bird. This is not an uncommon event for birders like me, but it is always stressful; my pulse shot up from the adrenaline rush. However, the birder claimed to have heard a response and was standing exactly where he had heard the bird the previous evening.

I set up my camera with a tripod and focused on the "open" areas in the nest of tangled vines where the bird might reveal itself. As the sun plunged toward the horizon, I began to hear the bird, accompanied by a Sora Rail, apparently its companion. As I concentrated on the origin of the sound, I was rattled by the sound of gunfire across the road. A group of teens arrived with ATVs, no more than 25 yards from where I stood. I waited for them to leave, but they showed no inclination to do so. The noise from the speedway continued as well. Finally, I walked to the group of teens and asked them, partially in Spanish, if they would consider moving a bit away from me since I was "trying to hear and film a very rare bird." I let them know that I didn't mean to decrease their fun. They were quite gracious and moved away—it is amazing how effective a little diplomacy can be.

As I watched and listened, I noticed movement in the reeds from which the calls continued, albeit quite intermittently. Suddenly, I spotted a tiny dark bird perched on the top of the reed tangle. It had not flown in but came from somewhere in the quagmire below. I got my camera on it and obtained two exposures, both blurry, but showing what appeared to be a tiny, mostly black bird with some small patches of white. I didn't have time to study the photos or enlarge them, but I determined to take a closer look once I got the opportunity. While all this was going on, I impulsively called Aura on FaceTime so she could see the whole scene of the impregnable snarl of reeds, hear the human cacophony, and maybe the call of the bird. She laughed and told me that I should hang up and concentrate on the task at hand. As always, I followed her "advice."

Finally, it was too dark to get any more photos, so I decided to return to Tucson in time to have sushi at my favorite place just down the street from my motel. I was elated to have heard the loud diagnostic call of the elusive and reclusive Ridgway's Rail and, perhaps, to have photographed something meaningful. I had seen this bird with Arnold Small in Newport Bay, California, when it used to be called the Clapper Rail before the split, and I felt comfortable with an auditory identification. I must also mention that, while I was talking to Aura, an American Bittern, a type of heron, flew into the reedbed and landed right where the rails were calling, perhaps part of an avian clique. It looked into the reeds, likely watching the rails. It didn't spook the rail but did seem to confirm its presence below, hidden (at least to me) in the foliage.

I drove back to Tucson, which took about two and a half hours, listening to Rachmaninov's "Variation on a Theme by Chopin." I arrived at my sushi place and found to my chagrin that it had been shut down by the pandemic. I had to settle for a Burger King Whopper, which seemed incongruous after my experience with the rail and Rachmaninov. While looking for the rail, I had texted Melody to confirm a pick-up time of 6 a.m. the next morning. She replied that maybe we should leave earlier. That is what I was hoping for after observing the times the flycatcher had been seen and reported. I responded that I would leave as early as she recommended.

I slept well but was jolted from sleep by a text from Melody at 4 a.m. asking if I was up and still open to the earlier start. I responded in the affirmative and we agreed to meet at 5:30. She promised muffins and hard-boiled eggs, and I had coffee in the room. I was at the door when she arrived, and we were an hour away from Life Bird 785 if things went well.

We were truly happy to see each other. It had been a few years, and at our advancing ages, you never know if you have seen someone for the last time. I presented Melody with a painting of the Tufted Flycatcher we had seen on my last visit, and with an accompanying palette abstract. She seemed very pleased and said she had a place for it on her wall and would send a photo once it was in place. I wolfed down muffins, a banana, and an egg, and drank coffee as we headed east to what turned out to be a beautiful low canyon along Paige Creek in the hills east of Tucson in Pima County.

As we drove, I had the opportunity to ask Melody about her husband, Eric, who was in hospice care the last time we had talked. He had died, as expected, about 18 months earlier of cerebrovascular disease. Melody and I talked about how much he had contributed to her successful business by shopping, driving, shuttling, and often waiting for hours. She had suffered a terrible loss and was still discovering things that Eric had done for her that now would not get done unless she did them herself. I had lost much in my two divorces, but had never faced the finality of the death of a spouse, a loss that can never be repaired.

We discussed the politics of Arizona, one of seven or eight polarized political swing states, more or less evenly split between Democrats and Republicans, with many highly controversial issues such as immigration and the conservation of its unique natural resources. Also known in the USA as purple states, these are the ones that determine the outcome of national elections. We also talked about her piano students. I was not aware of her celebrity as a pianist and teacher. She has several very talented young musicians and takes an enlightened, low-pressure approach. Melody is truly a woman for all seasons, who doesn't do anything unless she does it well. Getting to know her better was a highlight of this trip and something I had finally learned to do after missing the opportunity with several other guides and birders.

We arrived after about an hour on the road—and about an hour late.

At the site, we found several birders who told us that the Nutting's Flycatcher had been present and calling 30 minutes before our arrival but had flown further and further away and, ultimately, disappeared. Melody shook her head in frustration. Birding is getting more crowded and more difficult, especially when clients hire a renowned guide to find birds and, understandably, expect to find them. Of course, we should have left earlier, but she is now 74 years old, works nearly daily, and gets exhausted like everyone else. I knew we would be successful, but it might take all day.

We agreed on a strategy to wander a bit but stay close to the bird's favorite spot and hope for its likely but not guaranteed return. This strategy was the same strategy that Bob Buttery had used years before to locate my only Elegant Trogon in Cave Creek Canyon, just a short drive from where we were now. The keyword is patience—easier said than done. At least the Nutting's had been seen, so we knew it was around. As we waited, we watched as the other birders gradually left; we had the place to ourselves.

Within minutes, we heard the bird say: *Wheep!!* This was the diagnostic call we had hoped for and likely would not have heard if other birders had been present. Melody homed in quickly on the sound and indicated the bird's preference for the large sycamores along the nearly dry stream.

Then she said, as she had many times before in our joint ventures: "There! There he is!"

She was just as excited as I was; that says it all.

She pointed, I got my glasses on the bird, and I could see the characteristic features of its small dark head without much of a flycatcher crest, rusty wings and tail, and no band across the end of the tail. I got my camera on the bird and got several diagnostic photos.

Showing Melody what I had on my camera screen, she said, "That's the only decent photo anyone has gotten."

That was an exaggeration, but the photo did demonstrate the diagnostic features and preserved "my Nutting's" for me to revisit whenever I felt the need.

We were able to observe this rare bird for perhaps half an hour as it fed in trees and bushes and even on the ground. We were alone with the bird because we had been patient, the behavior for

Nutting's Flycatcher

which Melody is known and respected. The day was beautiful, as were the surroundings. We had a success hug and high fives. We agreed this was one experience that neither of us would forget. That is the way it can be when everything falls into place as a result of good planning: one life bird seen under ideal circumstances.

I would likely have missed it without Melody, who first heard the call and then quickly found the bird so I could get my photos. To see her so overjoyed, especially with her recent loss and after years of guiding, was inspirational. We agreed to savor the moment and limit what we did for the rest of our time. It was only 8 a.m., but the day had started with Melody's text at 4 a.m.

Seeing the Nutting's Flycatcher was one of those rare moments in life when you know you have experienced something transcendent, something indelible, and something that cannot be recreated. If you are in the moment, as we were, the experience becomes a memory so deeply imprinted that it will appear when least expected and always be welcome. To share such a moment with someone else who is like-minded makes it twice as powerful. That is when birding, which can devolve into a mechanical act of finding and checking off species, becomes a spiritual pursuit in the broadest sense of the term. The appropriate response to having the rare privilege of such an experience is gratitude—gratitude for the experience itself and for the effort and expertise required to make it possible. This experience added another piece to the puzzle of what drives birders to extremes that non-birders find so perplexing.

This had been one of my best birding days thanks to Melody, the Nutting's Flycatcher, and the beauty of Arizona's high desert.

The next morning, I drove to the airport and began to review my trip photos. I studied the attempts I had made to photograph whatever it was that I saw moving in the reeds that hid the Ridgway's Rail. I eventually came to suspect that I had filmed a Ridgway's Rail chick that looks like a black ball of fluff with a few odd white patches, but the photo was too blurry to be certain. Sometimes, persistence pays off if you persist in your persistence. (What do you think of that, Yogi?)

My life bird count stood at 784: "only" sixteen more to 800.

RULE 33
You can go home again.

Having sold our Denver loft and made significant progress in dealing with various health issues, we departed with a truck loaded with personal possessions we didn't want to entrust to the moving company, and set out to return to Canada. On the way, we planned a brief visit to Taos, New Mexico, where we would unwind and look at some prospective properties. We would continue our drive from Taos to Toledo, Ohio, where I grew up, to see some friends and console a high-school classmate, Sonya, who had just lost her spouse, Jim, another member of our class and a Vietnam veteran. I had presided over a few Zoom sessions to help her, him, and several classmates deal with the impending loss. Perhaps I had learned something about the value of friendship after all. We loaded up the truck and departed, bright and early, for Taos.

We took a long look at what had been our urban home since 2009, gulped back a few tears, and left Denver.

We were aware of some wildfires in New Mexico, but didn't realize until we got there how bad it was. People were being evacuated to Taos as we arrived there, and the air was smoky. Upon our arrival in Taos, we saw smoke and flames over the top of the mountains that separated the fire from Taos Valley. We decided to pack up and head east before things got worse. The specter of climate change and its effect on the natural world haunted our journey. When we started looking for a place to spend the night, and as the hour grew late, we discovered that everything was booked, probably by others fleeing the fire zone. We finally found marginal accommodations in, believe it or not, Dodge City, Kansas, more than three hours beyond where we wanted to stop and, ironically, only blocks from Boot Hill. Early the next morning, we got out of Dodge and drove to Toledo.

We drove from Kansas to the Dorr Street Café, on Dorr St. in Toledo, which is owned by my friend and high-school classmate, Bob Reichert. We were met by Bob, Sonya (who had flown from Atlanta for the occasion), and about a dozen other friends from my youth. We had a great time and cheered Sonya up as much as could be expected.

We ate fresh walleye from Lake Erie, arguably the most delectable of freshwater fishes. I picked up the tab for the whole gang, and we said our goodbyes. The next morning, I had breakfast with Sonya, and she came with Aura and me to visit the Historic Woodlawn Cemetery where my parents and grandparents are buried. The experience was emotional for all of us. We were getting old, losing loved ones, and doing our best to take care of one another. The burial site was in some disrepair. I had a brief conversation with the spirits of my family, arranged for the site to be restored, and departed.

Later that day, I drove to a wildlife refuge on the south shore of Lake Erie. A rare shorebird, a Curlew Sandpiper, had been reported the day before. I had never been to the area, which is only a 20-minute drive from the village of Ottawa Hills, where I lived until I went to college. When I arrived, I discovered hordes of birders. The parking lot was full, and I was told that no one had found the shorebird. I didn't find it either—no surprise—but I did see the refuge and many migratory birds that I had missed completely in the ignorance of my youth.

I felt good about discovering an aspect of Ohio that shed new light on the reality of where I had once lived. The Lake Erie region of northwestern Ohio is a mecca for birders who flock to the area during migration each year to experience the spectacle. The most famous place on Lake Erie to observe this is Point Pelee, in Ontario, where the exhausted birds rest after crossing the lake. Despite the fame of Point Pelee, I learned, better late than never, that the south shore of Lake Erie is a place where birders can see dozens of species of migratory birds in just one or two days.

Since I knew we would be passing through Ohio, I contacted a birder, Rick Sherwood, who lives in Sandusky, where my father had once kept his boat and where, in my high school days, I played saxophone in a rock band at the Peppermint Lounge. I asked if we might be able to find a Willow Flycatcher, a bird that was part of a split in which Traill's Flycatcher became Alder and Willow Flycatchers. When I meticulously reviewed my life list, I realized that I had never made the effort to locate this bird, which is scarce and endangered in Colorado. This was my chance to correct that oversight. This sighting was life bird 785, my only Ohio lifer, made possible years before when Traill's Flycatcher was split into Willow and Alder Flycatchers.

I finally got him on the phone, and he agreed to meet us in Sandusky early in the morning as we passed through on our way to New Jersey. We finally found him in a place that our GPS did not

Willow Flycatcher
Photograph by Steven McGrath

My Flycatcher Path in North America

seem to know about. He had been struck in the chest by a baseball while umpiring a game the night before and appeared to be in severe pain, but he was there nonetheless. He and I set out on a trail while Aura relaxed in the truck. We walked about a mile in a forested area near water that sounded like the birds' version of Beethoven's Ninth.

I deeply regretted that I couldn't linger, but we finally heard the diagnostic *fee-bee-oh* of the Willow Flycatcher, good enough for identification, since the appearance of the bird is exactly the same as the Alder Flycatcher. Moreover, I had seen it in Ohio, a place that I could now add to those places where I had seen life birds. This sighting was a confirmation, not a new bird, but confirmations like this are a necessity for serious listers. My list remained at 785, but the little Ohio bird filled a major gap. The following is a list of the journeys that were necessary to find the 42 species of flycatchers I have seen in North America.

***Arizona:** Vermilion Flycatcher, Greater Pewee, Sulfur-bellied Flycatcher, Buff-breasted Flycatcher, Ash-throated Flycatcher, Nutting's Flycatcher, Brown-crested Flycatcher, Rose-throated Becard, Tufted Flycatccher, Pine Flycatcher, Tropical Kingbirrd, Dusky-capped Flycatcher, Thick-billed Kingbird.*

***Texas**: Great Kiskadee, Social Flycatcher, Grey-collared Becard, Northern Beardless Tyrrranulet, Scissor-tailed Flycatcher, Couche's Kingbird, Great Crested Flycatcher*

Florida*: Grey Kingbird, LaSagra's Flycatcher, Great-crested Flycatcher*

Colorado: *Cordillerian Flycaatcher, Dusky Flycatcher, Olive-sided Flycatcher, Western Kingbird, Cassin's Kingbird, Hammond's Flycatcher, Eastern Kingbird, Fork-tailed Flycatcher, Say's Phoebe, Western Wood Pewee, Eastern Phoebe,)*

Ohio: *Willow Flycatcher*

Alaska: *Alder Flycatcher*

Georgia: *Acadian Flycatcher, Eastern Pewee*

California: *Grey Flycatcher, Pacific Slope Flycatcher, Black Phoebe*

Minnesota: *Yellow-bellied Flycatcher.*

After visiting my first daughter Jen and her two children in Plymouth, MA, we planned to stop at Revere Beach, which is just north of Boston's Logan Airport. I had been told by guide Tiffany Kersten that she had found Manx Shearwaters swimming there during her Big Year.

 *The Manx Shearwater is a handsome bird with a dark brown/ black mantle and facial markings, and white underwings and body. It nests primarily in northern Europe, especially near the Isle of Man, which lies between England and Ireland. The bird's name is derived from the name of this island, where the Manx Celtic language is being restored. There are scattered locations where small numbers of these shearwaters nest off the northern coast of North America, from Massachusetts to Newfoundland, but the birds scatter widely and, although not rare, are unpredictable.*

This shearwater had become a nemesis bird for me. I had little confidence that I would find it; it had been more than a year since

Tiffany had discovered it there. Nevertheless, it was on our way (more or less) and worth a try.

We found the beach easily, and it didn't look promising. It was late May, a warm day, and the beach was packed with people. I finally found a place to park, left Aura in the truck, and walked to a place where I could scan the semicircular beach with my binoculars. I spotted a flock of dark birds not more than a hundred yards from shore and very close to a bunch of human bathers wallowing in the waves. I could tell the birds were not ducks or geese, so I ran back to the truck to get my scope and camera. When I got the birds in focus, I was astonished to discover that I was looking at a flock of Manx Shearwaters, life bird 786.

I was able to relocate the flock in my camera by lining up a woman in heliotrope bloomers. The birds were just beyond where she stood, nearly motionless. They have the GISS of a seabird, streamlined with prominent sharp beaks.

 *GISS: A term that sounds worse than it is. It was probably derived from airplane identification during World War II in which the letters stood for General Impression of Size and Shape. In birding, the term more broadly means the impression that a bird gives of size, shape, behavior, flight, etc. This allows identification without being able to study the bird more carefully, or shooting it, which, despite Audubon, is generally frowned upon, especially by carrier pigeons, if they weren't extinct and if they could frown.*

These Manx shearwaters displayed a dark back, white underparts, and a white facial mask. While this was not the spiritual experience that I had in Arizona with Melody, it was indelible in other ways, and the presence of those birds was surreal. I later discovered that Massachusetts birders had designated this area as a birding "hot spot" because of the shearwaters, which probably nested on one of the offshore islands and took shelter in the protected harbor. To the best of my knowledge, this is the only place in North America where this pelagic species can be found reliably from shore.

Manx Shearwaters at Revere Beach,
Massachusetts, Life Bird 786

Revere Beach is also known locally for its "gourmet" hot roast beef sandwiches.

We arrived in Vermont later that day, where we met my daughter and her two boys at their lake house on Lake Champlain. We enjoyed seeing everyone, but we were ready to return to Unama'kik, our home by the sea in Cape Breton. The next morning, we headed for the Maine border, spent the night in Saint John, New Brunswick, and arrived the next afternoon in McNabs Cove. Despite finding the kitchen in shambles and unusable from incomplete renovations, we were finally, and undoubtedly, home. As expected, we were greeted by the cries and clicks of our guardian Bald Eagle, Winston, who reminded me, if just for a moment, of Stella, the now mythical Steller's Sea Eagle, last reported on the Avalon peninsula of Newfoundland, but seen by me only in my dreams.

PART 6

GREAT GREY OWL

> **RULE 34**
> With few exceptions, no goal is
> unobtainable until you decide it is.

After spending the previous two years in Nova Scotia, with some birding success as part of my life's most intimate time with nature, I resolved to sign up for tandem birding excursions in Alaska: the first to Barrow, now Utquiagvik, which is the northernmost point of the USA, and the second to Dutch Harbor in the Aleutian Islands, where "Deadliest Catch" is filmed. As it turned out, this arduous trip was tainted by unanticipated calamities. The first of these was a self-inflicted back injury which left me in pain for the entire journey. I had tried to lift my lawn tractor to remove some fabric that was wrapped around the blade. This proved that I still had a Y chromosome despite my advancing age.

The Dutch Harbor trip was primarily a pelagic trip into the Bering Sea in search of the Whiskered Auklet, the only Alaskan alcid,

Great Grey Owl   Red-necked Stint

which cannot be seen anywhere else. Alcids are a family of seabirds, including puffins, and sometimes called "the penguins of the north."

The birding tour company that I chose promoted the trip with an exciting video that showed the startling variety of birds that can be seen on this trip at sea, including the rare and resilient Short-tailed Albatross which, just a few years ago, faced extinction. I also expected to see Short-tailed Shearwaters, another life bird. What convinced me to sign up for this excursion was the clever guarantee that the pelagic trip was scheduled twice to reduce the risk of being skunked by foul weather. According to the tour information, the boat could accommodate only six birders plus a pilot and guide, and we would be almost guaranteed, on the journey to Utquiagvik, to see three spectacular species of eider ducks, with chances to see nesting and rare shorebirds, Snowy Owls, rare gulls, and polar bears.

On June 15, I arrived in Halifax. I planned to get some sleep before my Air Canada flight, which departed about 5 a.m. When the alarm rang at 3 a.m., I noticed a text that the flight was delayed until 10 a.m. because there was no pilot for the earlier departure. Instead of arriving in Anchorage at 2:30 p.m. with time to rest, I arrived at the Coast Inn at midnight, having crossed four time zones.

The next morning, I was exhausted and in pain, but I was with my group, excited, and on my way to Utquiagvik. The skies were clear, and the view from the plane revealed the dramatic transition from snow-covered peaks and frozen rivers to tundra, with thousands of frozen, iridescent Ice Age lakes, all looking uninhabited. When I caught my first glimpse of the north coast,

Land's End, I was overwhelmed with emotion. I had dreamed of this day for years, and my dream had been realized.

After checking into the only hotel in Utquiagvik, our group of about 16 people climbed into a van that was clearly past its prime and headed out birding. We were looking for a rare shorebird, the Red-necked Stint, which was being seen near the hotel. We arrived at a small pond on the main road along the Arctic Ocean, which was mostly frozen to the horizon. We scanned the pond and saw a few common shorebirds. As we walked around the pond, we spotted a smaller shorebird sporting conspicuous rusty red on its head and throat. It was the Red-necked Stint, my first life bird of the trip, number 787, and one that I had missed on a trip to Nome several years earlier. It was worth the wait.

I was able to get some photos once my hands stopped shaking. We also found some Steller's Eiders in open water off the coast, and spotted a small greenish bird in the tundra. We later identified it as an Arctic Warbler, not a rare bird in Alaska, but hundreds of miles from its usual haunts. We returned to the hotel and went to bed in broad daylight. I spent some time looking out the window at the frozen sea, hoping for an evening visit by a polar bear or a rare Ivory or Ross's Gull. No such luck, but I found it exciting just to be in a remote place where such observations were possible.

The next day, we had a hearty breakfast that included my choice of reindeer sausage.

 *I ordered those sausages every day thereafter. I still haven't figured out why it is called reindeer sausage rather than caribou sausage. It is the same animal, called caribou in North America and reindeer in Eurasia.*

We set out in the van to a road—the only road—where we hoped to find Steller's, King, and Spectacled Eiders, the principal target birds of the trip. We eventually reached another road that our guide hoped to explore, but he determined that it was too wet and muddy for our van. He told us that our permit to drive the few roads around Utquiagvik did not allow us to walk on the tundra where we might have found other ponds and more birds. This was the first knowledge I had of this restriction or the limitations we faced because of our vehicle and the size of our group.

Steller's Eiders
These are in the Arctic Ocean

Spectacled Eider, Life Bird 788
Too Far Away for a Good Photograph

We saw many breeding birds we expected to see, but eiders were scarce. We finally found a few Steller's Eiders and one pair of King Eiders, but no Spectacled Eiders. Finally, we spotted a solitary birder squatting on the roadside, taking photos. Our guide, who had shown no signs of concern, wisely stopped the van and asked the photographer, who had probably organized his own trip, what he was seeing. He tersely replied, "A pair of Spectacled Eiders." We courteously moved our van a safe distance before unloading to have a look. The pair of eiders was at least 700 yards away. The guide got the birds quickly in his scope so we could line up for a quick view in case they spooked.

One member of our group, an elderly and Eeyore-like woman, complained, "I can't really see the birds at that distance, and as far as I'm concerned, I haven't seen them." Despite her negativity, I understood her feelings. I got a pretty good look and some poor photos that were only adequate for identification, but we had come to the top of the world to see this bird. As it turned out, that was our only look. We spotted one Snowy Owl that was too far away to photograph. No other rarities were found, including rare gulls.

And we didn't see a polar bear.

Still, I had two life birds and many good photos of nesting birds in brilliant breeding plumage, including gorgeous Pacific Loons. Most birders see these loons in dull winter coats, but in my view, they are among the world's most handsome birds in full breeding plumage.

King Eider drake

This spectacular drake was probably 500 yards from the road. I had seen one before off Montauk, New York, circa 1972.

Pacific Loons

Red Phalarope
I had Only Seen these at Sea in Flight

My favorite loon; I had seen others, but never in breeding plumage. The red eyes don't show well in this distant photo.

Utqiagvik International Airport
Including the Interchangeable
Entrance and Exit Doors

The next day was foggy with light rain and poor visibility. We drove the same roads without anything new, then traipsed around disrespectfully in an old Indigenous cemetery looking for birds I had seen before. I declined the afternoon's birding to get some rest and, as I expected, the group found nothing else. The fog persisted, and a flight with more birders coming from Anchorage was canceled. We faced the risk of our return flight also being canceled, which would have impacted the flight from Anchorage to Dutch Harbor and put our pelagic trip in jeopardy.

It occurred to me as I rested that our time would have been better spent exploring the highly regarded Inuit Museum or some of the local environmental research facilities. We might have visited with some of the Indigenous elders to hear about their histories and lives. These options were neither discussed nor offered.

On the last day, we were out birding again. Once we were a mile or two away from the town, the fog cleared but remained stationary and ominously thick over the airport. By the time we reached a road that we hadn't explored, our time had run out. Maybe we would have found some closer eiders there, but we'll never know.

We got to the airport for our departure. Inside the small, antiquated building, maskless travelers were standing shoulder to shoulder. There was no place for the arriving passengers to walk without elbowing their way out, as we had done when we arrived. Since I had thought ahead and hadn't checked a bag, I could get out into the fresh air. COVID was still an issue, and Alaska is notorious for anti-vaxers. The chaotic scene at the airport leaves an unpleasant memory of Barrow. The addition of one room to the airport would solve this problem and quickly pay for itself by increasing tourism.

We boarded our plane and had an uneventful flight to Anchorage. I would fly to Dutch Harbor the next day. On the plane, I sat next to a professor of biology from Fairbanks. I chatted with him about my experience. He told me that he had guided a small group of students from the University and that they had been able, in a small SUV, to get off the main road and see numerous eiders at close range. He also told me that, with a smaller vehicle, there was the option, late at night in the midnight sun, to travel to Point Barrow, where the residents leave the carcasses of slaughtered whales and walruses. Here is where there is a reasonable possibility of spotting a polar bear or an Ivory Gull, both of which like to scavenge dead animals. Our vehicle was too large and heavy to get there, so we missed this opportunity. This is also where we hoped to find nesting Buff-breasted Sandpipers. I felt let down and disappointed as I flew toward my next destination. What next?

We arrived in Anchorage and checked into the Coast Inn. This was the only night of lodging in Anchorage covered in our contract, although I needed lodging the nights before and after the tours. The next day, we flew to Dutch Harbor, about three hours over the Aleutians with knockout views of the volcanic islands and mountains. We descended into Unalaska, the island where the town of Dutch Harbor (and its harbor) is located. As we banked sharply to line up our landing, we got close views of the verdant cliffs and waterfalls surrounding the town. It looked like Kauai with snow. I had never seen anything more spectacular.

The airport was small but much more satisfactory than Barrow's. The first thing I saw after deplaning was a sign that said, *Welcome to Dutch Harbor. The nearest doctor is 800 miles away.* Alaskan humor, I guess. We were greeted by our second guide. We divided the group of twelve in half, each with its own guide. We would eat together, but we would do all our birding separately, including the crucial pelagic trip. I did the math and quickly concluded that the concept of having two opportunities to get on a boat that had a capacity of six birders was not possible even with the New Math.

Our group would go out the next day, come hell or high water, or both. If we were unable to sail, we would not see a Whiskered Auklet, the reason we had come and for which we had paid dearly. No one brought this up. The weather report was favorable, and we

Whiskered Auklet, Life Bird 789
My Best Effort

Laysan Albatross

were coming out of a godawful pandemic, so we were optimistic. As it turned out, both groups were able to get out, but if we had not, or if one group had an experience superior to the other, there would have been some disgruntled people. At least birders seldom resort to violence.

The next morning, we boarded our seaworthy boat on calm seas with good visibility. We cruised the shores on the way out to look for Kittlitz's Murrelets and got just one brief and uncertain look. This was one of my life bird targets. About an hour later, we approached the Baby Islands, the nesting grounds of the Whiskered Auklets. Soon, we encountered flocks of these smallish birds flying over the water. Some were in the water but became quickly spooked as the boat approached. I was able to see their characteristic facial pattern and stubby red bills, but got just one photograph that identified the bird. Inexplicably, we made no effort to find this rare bird perching on the islands where it nests, nor did we stop the boat so that the auklets would not flush.

We were dazzled by hundreds of Tufted and a few Horned Puffins. There were also thousands of Northern Fulmars, a large gull-like seabird, mostly in the dark phase, but there were also a few handsome light-phase birds. Now, it was time to head for deeper water in search of albatrosses and a chance to see a rare Short-tailed Albatross.

We arrived in deep water and spotted an occasional Laysan Albatross, so we stopped and started chumming with buckets of ripe, oily bait fish. It wasn't long before we were visited by numerous Laysan Albatrosses, which breed on Midway Island of World War

Red-legged Kittiwake   Northern Fulmar, Light Phase

ll fame, and a few larger Black-footed Albatrosses. We also had a few gorgeous white-phase Northern Fulmars. These majestic seabirds were at close range and often in the wake of the boat. The highlight of this part of the journey was a Red-footed Kittiwake, in my opinion the most enchanting of gulls. It is normally found only on St. Paul Island in the Bering Sea, where I had seen it years before.

Speaking of gulls, most people, even some birders, use the term seagull when referring to gulls. The use of this invented word is not only incorrect but an egregious redundancy, like yellow jaundice, global pandemic, sugar diabetes, spinal meningitis, tiger cat, or popular vote. Moreover, the word seagull is pejorative to gulls, a large and diverse family of birds found nearly everywhere on earth and identified correctly and mellifluously as Heermann's Gull, Swallow-tailed Gull, Black-legged Kittiwake, etc.

Many birders do not like gulls. True, gulls are noisy, aggressive, and more than willing to steal your lunch if given the opportunity. Their colors, except the rare Ross's Gull which has a pink hue on its body, are restricted to shades of white, black, and grey, although the legs and beak may have brighter colors. Because of their restricted coloration and the fact that it takes three or four years to reach adult plumage, they are difficult and frustrating to identify. I am a gull supporter and enjoy the challenge of correctly identifying them (even if they do not require or seek my support). I admire animals with the intelligence and personality of gulls and their propensity for mischief. I feel the same way about disobedient dogs—as long as I don't get bitten or blamed for their havoc.

205

Kittlitz's Murrelets, Life Bird 791

While we were enjoying the spectacle of hundreds of birds encircling our boat, I noticed a large fish-processing vessel a few miles away. I remembered that seabirds congregate around these ships and how much this had improved my pelagic experience in Oregon, the experience that inspired me to write this book. Could there have been a Short-tailed Albatross near the ship? We will never know.

Finally, a few Short-tailed Shearwaters flew past our boat, but I had expected to see hundreds. That bird, and the Whiskered Auklet, were life birds 789 and 790. I was elated, of course, but concerned about other birds that might have been missed on this tour. I am still burdened by doubts about the commitment of the guides to providing the best outcome for their clients.

We were served a hearty soup and excellent bread made by the skipper in his cozy warren, where he could control the boat, listen to music, and cook. We returned to Dutch Harbor after an excellent day in the unusually comfortable Bering Sea. The other group of birders was able to do their pelagic trip the next day and found all the desired birds, but nothing else, while our group searched the shores around Dutch Harbor for Kittlitz's Murrelets, which we hadn't seen on the boat.

I was told, perhaps a bit late to allay my anxiety, that our chances of seeing it were better from shore. We finally found a few of these birds, which are much less common than the abundant Marbled and Ancient Murrelets. This was life bird 791 and a great relief, since I thought my only chance to see it was on the pelagic trip.

Having completed our spectacular visit to Dutch Harbor, we went to the airport and boarded our flight on RAVN Airlines without any boarding zones or security checks. The three-hour flight took us past Mount Denali, of which we had a spectacular view, and we landed shortly thereafter. Half of us were on a later flight, so I thanked our guide and said my farewells to the others before taking the shuttle to the Coast Inn.

After a stressful evening trying to get a boarding pass, I arrived at the airport at noon for my 3 p.m. flight and was able to get to the gate. I departed on Air Canada for Halifax and arrived at about 4 p.m. Atlantic Time, about 20 hours after leaving Anchorage. My wife had already arrived at our inn near the airport. We were elated to be reunited and had a celebratory martini.

This epic experience had taken me across North America and to the northernmost place in the United States. I had seen five life birds, and they had not come easily. I was physically unprepared for such a demanding journey and was in constant pain from my careless back injury. Most of the last hours in Alaska, which should have been spent basking in my experience, were spent desperately trying to manage the intricacies of the technical world that belonged to the generations of my children and grandchildren.

About a month after my return from Alaska, I learned that Stella, the elusive Steller's Sea Eagle, had been discovered roosting on a cliff in Trinity Bay, Newfoundland. Local whale-watching boats were taking birders to see her daily. I booked myself on the ferry from North Sydney to Argentia, Newfoundland, found a place to stay in Trinity Bay, about a two-hour drive from the ferry port, and a spot on one of the boats that would look for the eagle. When it was time to go, my post-COVID symptoms had intensified, and Aura was not game for this journey after her own COVID infection and her discomfort with boats. I canceled the trip with the sinking feeling that I had probably missed my last chance to see Stella.

In November 2022, I made a plan to meet my daughter Jennifer in St. Andrews, New Brunswick, which is exactly the midpoint between my home in Cape Breton and hers in Plymouth, Massachusetts. We would enjoy some rare time together without any distractions, and she would deliver medication to me that could not be shipped across the border. We met on the Sunday after American Thanksgiving and arrived, more or less simultaneously, at the historic Algonquin Resort, a well-preserved Tudor-style hotel.

After dinner by the fire and a bottle of Chablis, we relaxed in our room, where I checked the New Brunswick rare bird alert. Much to my shock, I discovered that earlier that day, and only an hour out of my way, Stella had been seen and photographed on the Gulf of St. Lawrence near Cormier-Village, New Brunswick. I knew I had missed the eagle again, but Jennifer was adamant that we should go the next day and take our chances.

We departed after breakfast on a windy, cold, and drizzly day. We arrived three hours later, found a few inveterate shivering birders with whom we commiserated, looked around for an hour, then drove back to St. Andrews. We had tried, but Stella was gone—probably on her way south. Ironically, the name of the only boat docked in the eagle-less harbor was the Stella B. Despite the absence of Stella, the eagle, Jen and I had a memorable day together.

The eagle was no longer just a bird to me. Rather, it had become synonymous with my own unanswered and, perhaps, unanswerable questions. From Golden Eagles in Colorado to our guardian Bald Eagle in Cape Breton, and now a Steller's Sea Eagle haunting Atlantic Canada, eagles had shared many important milestones of my life with no apparent explanation and have become, in the process, my spiritual animus.

Sea Eagle Stella

You arrived in Gaspé
in a pandemic spring
all the way from Siberia
you somehow flew

to Windsor, Nova Scotia
where you stayed for a day
and where I first sought you
only two hours late.

Then Bristol, Massachusetts
where the Wampanoag lived
and Booth Bay, Maine
Where I missed you again.

You vanished again
in April and May
but turned up again
in Trinity Bay, where

I missed you again.
COVID stopped me this time
then Shediak,, New Brunswick
late again by a day.

And so, my fair Stella
you´ve become so much more than
A bird to be found
A bird to be seen.

You´re the winged incarnation
of what I still seek
what I still need
but cannot obtain.

You grasp in your talons
my soul, not a fish
and answers to questions
I might never know, like:

Where did you come from?
Where are you going?
When will I find you?
And what if I don´t?

RULE 35

While the day is fast approaching when we will not know if we are dealing with a human or a bot, wild birds are the real thing.

I t was February 2024, and I was preparing myself for back surgery for painful sciatica, which had fortunately responded well to two injections of steroids and local anesthesia. I checked the Texas eBird rare bird alert, as I do religiously, and discovered that there were at least eight birds there I had never seen—a bonanza, but a long and arduous trip from deep-winter Nova Scotia, where we had just had six feet of snow.

After my last trip to Alaska, I had decided to avoid long wild-bird chases, but I lost my resolve. I checked with Irina, my Russian travel agent, who is used to my impulsive birding escapades. We concluded that I was better off driving to Boston and flying from there—half the price and a much more reasonable one-stop itinerary. I gulped a few times, consulted with my spouse, as always, and decided to test myself yet again. I contacted my previous fine guide, Tiffany Kersten, who made some arrangements for me with something less than full disclosure and none of the warmth I had anticipated as a repeat customer. It seemed to me that the world, in general, was less friendly in these divided and scary times.

One of the birds was a fantastic rarity, a Mottled Owl, never seen before in North America. Seeing the bird required a guided group tour into the private Santa Margarita Ranch, which is on the Rio Grande River, about a 90-minute drive from Alamo, where I always stay. I consulted several people who guide on the Ranch, but they did not tell me the night walk for the owl is often booked weeks in advance. I scheduled a day tour to see the Bare-throated Tiger Heron, but I was skunked on the night tour—and thus the owl. I didn't know about that until I finally spoke with my guide, who gave me the bad news and sent an email address for me to try to persuade the only guide who leads the owl tours to include me. My email was met with sincere regrets, but no admission to the tour. I responded shamelessly, hoping that my age might be considered or maybe someone would cancel.

The Santa Margarita Ranch is located between a section of ghastly monolithic border wall and the serene Rio Grande River. We walked about a half mile to a bluff with a panoramic view of the river, where we saw a variety of wildlife, including a family of bobcats and two Limpkins, large wading birds in the rail family that had always been limited to Florida but turned up in Texas that year. I had only seen one before. As we scanned the river, the two Limpkins flew toward us, feasting on clams for at least an hour.

We also saw the rare Green and Ringed Kingfishers that inhabit the Rio Grande River. I had seen those birds before, but they are always a treat and very colorful as they fly up and down the river looking for fish and vocalizing to each other. Our guide spotted a Hook-billed Kite soaring across the river. We all got good looks. This was an unexpected bird, a nemesis bird that I had looked for without success numerous times, but finally spotted on a previous visit to Texas. This was a much better look. These birds of prey feed exclusively on a small tree snail. When the snails are prevalent in wet years, the birds are more common and can sometimes be found on their feeding grounds. Otherwise, seeing one depends on a flyover, which is never predictable. They have a sharply hooked yellow bill, broad wings that are narrower near the body, and a long, striped tail. All this was wonderful, but something was missing: the Bare-throated Tiger Heron, our extremely rare and desirable target bird. Eventually, we left our location to look elsewhere, feeling anxious that the bird might have departed. I had missed it several years earlier, arriving one day too late.

We drove to a more remote area of the ranch and walked for hours in the intensifying heat. I drank four bottles of water and still felt dehydrated. I had gone from sub-freezing temperatures in Nova Scotia to the high 90s Fahrenheit. We stopped for a break at a spot famous for Brown Jays, which had been absent from the Valley for many years. They are the world's largest jays, nearly the size of a raven, and very raucous. Our guide decorated the area with oranges, marshmallows, and watermelon. As we watched, this Christmas tree of treats was attacked by Brown Jays, spectacular Green Jays, Altamira Orioles, and a Clay-colored Thrush (formerly Clay-colored Robin), which I had seen just once before.

I managed to get a few good photos, then we headed for the water. We had some clogs to wear as we crossed the water to an island in the Rio Grande that was probably in Mexico, but I won't tell. Once on the island, we spotted the elusive Bare-throated Tiger-

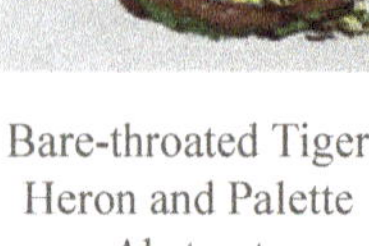

Bare-throated Tiger
Heron and Palette
Abstract

Hook-billed Kite

Heron at a distant spot up the river. We could see it, but the view was suboptimum. Nevertheless, we were thrilled and very mindful that we would have missed it without our trusty guide. We trudged our way back to our cars, feeling a bit weathered but exhilarated. The heron was life bird 792. The hike out made me think of the Bataan Death March, but I survived to make the long drive back to Alamo, where I passed out at 7 p.m. with the ubiquitous Tex-Mex food in my belly.

I was up at 5 a.m., and on my way to Resaca de La Palma Reserve to meet my next guide. I had him to myself for the day. Our targets at the reserve were a Roadside Hawk, a raptor that regularly strays from Mexico, and oddly enough, prefers to roost on roadsides where it hunts for prey that are scared up by traffic, and a Grey-collared Becard, a new flycatcher for North America. Our guide, a student at UTRGV, had a keen ear and could hear and identify birds that most clients could not. We found the Roadside Hawk quite easily, lifer 793, roosting in its usual spot on the roadside. It is nice, once in a while, to find a bird quickly and where it is supposed to be.

The becard was a different story. It forages constantly, and a birder must wait until the bird decides to show up. Finally, after searching for a couple of hours, during which we had good looks at Tropical Parula Warblers, I noticed a group with their glasses aimed at some trees in the parking area. We hustled to the group and immediately spotted the becard. It is not uncommon to find a bird because others have found it first. The Grey-collared Becard had the large triangular head of a flycatcher; its head was black and stood out against its grey

Altamira Oriole

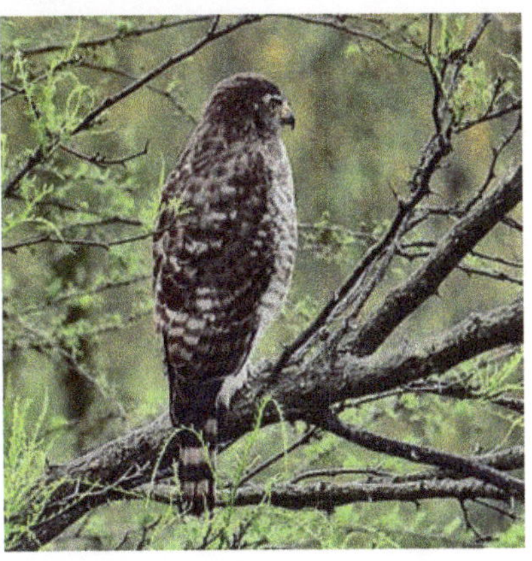

Roadside Hawk, Life Bird 793
Perched at the Roadside with its
Long, Striped Tail and Yellow Bill

neck and belly—a very handsome bird and lifer 794. We were both relieved to find this prize, which can be elusive.

Collar: The part of a bird below the head where a collar might be if birds wore shirts. Birds seldom dress up, and I would give the shirt off my back if someone could think of a better name.

We drove to the University of Texas Rio Grande Valley campus, the same place where I had seen the Social Flycatcher with Tiffany two years before. The campus is beautiful, with large trees, flowers, bridges over the resaca, and a plethora of good birds. Many of the students are Latino. It was uplifting to see these young members of an ethnic group that is caught in a political conflict enjoying college life.

My guide, a student at UTRGV, does bird guiding instead of being a teaching assistant to help with his expenses. He is the one who discovered the Fan-tailed Warbler that we hoped to find. He had documented its pattern of behavior and identified the best place to find it. This meant sitting on the ground and looking down into a poorly lit path beside a tangle of dense vegetation. The bird stays on the ground and passes by this spot once or twice a day. If you are there at the right time, you will see it. We weren't and didn't. It had been seen at 7 a.m. that day when we were elsewhere. There were many herons

Grey-Collared Becard, Life Bird 794
Photograph Provided by Evan Farese

Fan-tailed Warbler, Life Bird 795
Photograph Provided by Evan Farese
Who Discovered this Rarity

and interesting waterfowl in the water near our spot to provide some consolation, as well as flocks of Green Parakeets. We finally gave up. It was mid-afternoon, and my guide felt guilty. I told him to relax and not worry. I would return early the next day, as he recommended, to look some more.

The next morning, I was back on campus at the warbler stakeout at 7 a.m. I was soon joined by a nice woman and an older man. The woman, Cheryl, had been the one to spot the becard the day before. She was confident about our chances and told me that she would be on the owl tour that night. She suggested that I send one last plaintive email, which I did as we waited. At 8:39, I looked to the left of where a Long-billed Thrasher was digging for bugs and spotted a smaller bird approaching on the ground no more than five feet from where I sat. After a good look, I said, "That's it!" and there he was. A small plump bird with a dark back and a yellow-orange belly with several small white marks around the face. The dark tail had a white tip. It was our Fan-tailed Warbler. I had forgotten to put a battery in my camera, but managed a decent photo with my cellphone. Seconds later, our avian friend was gone.

Cheryl was overjoyed; this was her 600th life bird. John Trochet, our other companion, said that this was the only species of warbler he hadn't seen in North America. I facetiously asked him if he had seen Bachmann's Warbler, which went extinct in the early 1970s. I was shocked when he said, "Yes, I was one of the last to see it in a swamp near Charleston, South Carolina." Ironically, I had been living nearby in Augusta, Georgia at the time.

John is about my age, and it occurred to me that when he passes on, there won't be anyone left who has seen Bachmann's Warbler. I have never met anyone else who has seen it. John told me he would mention my name in his posting since I had spotted the Fan-tailed Warbler first. He also said he was part of a group of biologists who published a recent paper attesting to the survival of a few Ivory-billed Woodpeckers in Louisiana. Most believe the bird to be extinct, but he has photos, recordings, and a visual identification of the bird. John gave me the citation for his paper, and we all exchanged contact information and went our separate ways.

I decided to go to Laguna Atascosa Refuge to look for a Blue Bunting that had last been seen six days earlier. I missed this difficult vagrant years before when it flew in front of me and disappeared before I could put my binoculars on it. On the way, I encountered an Aplomado Falcon doing its characteristic hovering act as it watches for prey. This was a much better look at this bird than my only previous look. Once extinct in North America, it is now on its way back, thanks to the conservation efforts of people like Evan, who have chosen a crucial but non-lucrative career in wildlife biology. I spent three hours at Laguna and never found the bunting. I was disappointed, but I had the other new lifers to provide consolation. I arrived at my room in Alamo ready to relax and take a break from birding.

But then I checked my email.

I was shocked to see that at the last minute, I had been invited to join the owling group. I would have to leave in 15 minutes and drive nearly two hours to get there in time. I hesitated but reasoned that I would never forgive myself if I missed that bird, the rarest of the Texas lot. I took off in a few minutes and raced to the site.

I arrived on time to meet a group of about 25 avid birders, including Cheryl. We had two guides, Simon and Zach, who were highly skilled and had all the necessary equipment, including an infrared device to locate birds at night, an ultra-bright directional light, and a tape with all the necessary calls. We were given explicit instructions on how to behave to improve our chances. We must be silent and use lights only if necessary to avoid falling. We would walk about two miles in the dark and look for other birds and owls as well as the Mottled Owl.

*This session reminded me of my legendary high school teacher, Coach Norman Neidermeier, who famously announced on the first day of school each year, "There's only one rule. You can't do nuthin'!"*

Simon suggested that the group was large because there was a birder or two who begged their way into the tour. I wanted to hide somewhere. To change the subject, I told one of the birders, a tall, middle-aged man, about my failed effort to find a Blue Bunting that day. He bragged about how he had found it by spending many hours roaming the area of its first discovery and told me that I hadn't spent enough time looking. In other words, it was my fault. The truth was that the bird hadn't been seen for six days (and hadn't been seen since). Birders who seem to enjoy making other birders miserable are uncommon, but always seem to come out of the woodwork when an opportunity arises. This is one of the regrettable behaviors of birders that I described earlier, one that contrasts starkly with the collegiality of my two fellow observers of the Fan-tailed Warbler.

We began our trek, which took us through the lugubrious iron wall into the wilderness on the other side. The spotlights helped us to find our way. After about a half hour trek, we stopped and listened in silence as the mist descended. Everyone behaved; there was much at stake. We heard the primal call of Common Pauraques, a nightjar related to Whip-poor-wills and Nighthawks. Finally, we heard a few hoots from the Mottled Owl, a sound we had memorized during our instructions. Our trusty leaders figured out where the bird was with the infrared device, gave us a warning gesture to set our cameras, and beamed the intense light at an adjacent tree. The owl, life bird number 796, was sitting calmly on a heavy horizontal branch in plain sight. Its call reminded me that I had heard this owl in Guatemala while climbing Volcan Guadalupe at night as we watched the eruption of Volcan Fuego across Lake Atitlan.

No one said a word, but many camera shutters clicked. The owl lingered and then dropped out of sight. A few minutes later, and further down the trail, he reappeared and put on another show. The bird is large, about the size of a Spotted Owl. It has dark eyes, a brown back with white mottling, a white belly with brown vertical streaks, and a striking white stripe that begins on the brow and encircles the eyes before descending along the beak to the neck. Its hoot is loud

The Wall in
Santa Margarita Ranch

Mottled Owl, Life Bird 796 - Photograph
Provided by Zachary Johnson

and comes in groups of three to five. We needed to get away to avoid stressing the bird, but no matter where we went, it followed us and responded to any other bird call or even the leader's voice with more hoots. We were forced to leave the area and finally heard some other owls very faintly. Finally, we were far enough away to find an Eastern Screech Owl, which also gave us a show. I patted Cheryl on the back, happy she had such a great day and that I could share her joy. The adventure was over, or so I thought.

As the great-grandson of Jewish Lithuanian and Hungarian immigrants, I do not think this wall sends the right message.

I began the long drive back to Alamo with an ETA of midnight. I needed to leave early the next day for the airport. I was stopped by a police officer in Pharr, Texas, for going 40mph in a 30mph zone. The speed limits change so frequently that a well-placed officer can catch a lot of people. I was repentant and friendly, and when he asked why I had rented the car, I told him about my birding. The officer decided to give me a warning—the second time I had averted a citation because I was a birder. I don't recommend speeding, but if you must, you should consider carrying some birding gear instead of having a bumper sticker that says, "Eat My Dust."

After driving away from the police officer, I got lost because of construction that had started while we were owling, and I didn't arrive in Alamo until about 1 a.m.

 *Owling: The name given to the practice of benighted birders who venture out on a dark night, usually in February or March, when owls are most vocal, in hopes of finding and/or counting owls who can see in the dark whilst birders cannot.*

On my way back to Boston, I had a three-hour layover in Houston. I stubbornly refused to eat anything that required the robotic QR code ordering system. Instead, I found a sandwich place where I could order and pay a human—at least he looked human. I suppose there will come a day when I can be fooled about that too, but birds are still birds, at least when encountered in the wild. I guess that is the lesson of this trip.

I was now within four birds of 800.

A RARE BIRD IN THE CAPE BRETON HIGHLANDS, LIFER 797, BICKNELL'S THRUSH, JULY 13, 2024

When I arrived in Cape Breton in 2020, I learned that Cape Breton Highlands National Park is the northern edge of the Adirondack Mountains and thus of the Appalachians. I also learned that Bicknell's Thrush, one of the rarest of North American birds, nests there in small numbers.

I missed this bird in the Dry Tortugas years before when I left the spot where it was seen to explore another area. I had seen it briefly, albeit without photographic or vocal confirmation, at the top of Whiteface Mountain in upstate New York in autumn, when it was silent. Now I could hear it sing and perhaps get a look, but the bird is so rare and the terrain so challenging, that it took four years to find someone to help me find it.

The park is just a part of the Cape Breton Highlands, which tower above the sea and form the spine of a peninsula that extends northeast from the rest of Cape Breton. This is where explorer John Cabot is believed to have made the first landfall in North America since the Vikings. The terrain rises sharply from the Gulf of St. Lawrence on the north side and the Gulf of Maine to the south. The highest peaks extend above the tree line and are inhabited by a population of moose that are the last known in Cape Breton and possibly the mainland of Nova Scotia as well.

There are scattered locations where Bicknell's Thrush can be found. The best-known location is Money Point, which is outside the park boundaries near the peninsula's tip. Sightings have been rare, even though audio surveillance indicates the species is present. My friend, Steve McGrath, a native "Caper" and superb naturalist and photographer, is an explorer who often leaves the established trails to roam his native island in search of rare birds and plants—or just for adventure. On one such occasion, he followed an old moose trail to a ridge from which he could see both Cape Breton coasts. As he walked the trail for about a kilometer, the habitat changed from dense scrub forest to an open treeless ridge with mostly rocks, moss, and lichens. After the first half, he began hearing the song of the Bicknell's

Ruffed Grouse

Bicknell's Thrush
Photograph Provided by Steven McGrath

Thrush—a whirring vibrato, similar to the song of the Veery, another thrush.

Steve heard several of these birds as he continued to the end, where the terrain fell sharply on both sides. He was rewarded with a few glimpses of the rare thrush as it perched and sang on top of one of the stunted conifers. Eventually, he was able to get some good photographs. Since that day, he has returned many times, and, in June and July when the thrush is nesting, he has always found the bird. I asked Steve to either take me there or provide me with directions. He graciously agreed to go on July 13, 2024, despite the predicted high temperatures and humidity.

I rose at 3:30 a.m. and brought a thermos of coffee and some of Aura's delicious homemade bagels. The only thing I forgot was my hat. I arrived at Steve's house in Sydney at 5:45, and we set out for the Highlands. We drove to Englishtown, where a ferry would save us some driving time by crossing the Bras d'Or Lake. We exited the ferry on the Cabot Trail, the illustrious road that circumnavigates the entire peninsula. The road, which often reaches at least a ten percent grade, is a destination for road cyclists like I once was.

We left the Cabot Trail after passing through the charming town of Ingonish and headed toward Meat Cove. We turned off the paved road onto a gravel road that climbed steeply. Steve told me this road had been improved substantially and had once been nearly non-navigable. This is probably why so few people were aware of its extraordinary population of birds. We came to a spot where a Styrofoam buoy hung from a branch that marked the trailhead. As I pulled over to park the truck, a Ruffed Grouse with a single chick walked out of the weeds where we could take photographs. Unfortunately, the obedient chick quickly disappeared into the foliage while the mother stayed on the road to distract us.

We gathered our gear, including a satellite GPS that Steve carries to avoid getting lost in the woods. His version of this piece of equipment also allows him to get audio recordings of birds and provides a quantitative estimate of the accuracy of the identification. This innovative technology is yet another example of the variety of new devices that aid birders and naturalists in their zeal to make accurate identifications and live to tell their stories.

Before starting our trek, Steve played a recording of Bicknell's song and alarm call to prepare me, then we struck out on a wet but mostly flat trail. After about 15 minutes, Steve stopped and smiled. I listened and was able to hear the song of our bird, but I doubt that I would have identified it correctly without Steve or my Merlin audio bird app. I took a screenshot of my phone, which displayed the Merlin report confirming I had just heard my first Bicknell's Thrush. This solidified the thrush's spot on my life bird list, number 797.

As we walked this trail, which was so luxuriant that I imagined myself in the time of the dinosaurs, we stopped often to observe the unique flora, which included several rare species of orchids with wonderful names like Checkered Rattlesnake Plankton. Steve confirmed the correct species on his device. It's a new world, not always better, but in the case of these technologies, better. Giving something beautiful a name adds to its beauty and enhances the memory.

We were able to get a brief glimpse of the Bicknell's Thrush and could see its brownish body, finely streaked breast, and orange mandible. There was too much wind for it to perch and sing, and it was perhaps a little late in the season. We continued our hike to the end of the trail, where we sat on a soft bed of moss and listened. We heard more Bicknell's Thrushes and other birds, but we were sitting in a cloud that shielded us from the heat and humidity below, while obscuring our view of the birds. We sat for a while in this pleasant place where I could only imagine the stunning views of the terrain and the sea below that Steve described to me. Eventually, we reluctantly hiked out and encountered the same Bicknell's Thrush on our way out that we had heard before.

We explored another trail, more of a moose track than a trail. As we began to explore this sketchy hike, Steven stated in a revealing monotone, "We are going somewhere." We didn't find any more thrushes, but did find a Noah's Ark of bugs and saw some monstrous tracks of a moose with its calf. I was wearing a hat that I borrowed from Steve, so he could find me if I sank into quicksand. I had just seen life bird 797, not a good time to perish in a bog of moose droppings.

RULE 37
Dreams can come true, and the truth
can be as good as the dream.

Stella, the Steller's Sea Eagle, perhaps the most coveted and pursued wild bird of all time in North America, had spent the last two summers in Trinity Bay, Newfoundland. She was spotted several times during the winter and spring in western coastal Newfoundland and returned to Trinity Bay in June. She was seen nearly daily from tour boats a few miles from the town of Trinity. I monitored her from afar through the daily reports on eBird, which said she was building a nest high on a sea cliff while she waited, in vain, for a mate that would never come.

I began to plan yet another attempt to see this spectacular and elusive nemesis bird, but flights from Halifax to St. John's were prohibitively expensive. The overnight ferry from North Sydney, Nova Scotia, to Argentia, Newfoundland, would get me within a three-hour drive of Trinity Bay, but the ferry was in dry dock for repairs. The other ferry to Port aux Basques, Newfoundland, was operational and a much shorter trip, but its destination was more than 800 kilometers from the bird. That would mean spending two full days in the car, a big ask for my wife, since we could spend only one full day in Trinity Bay. So, I booked the ferry to Argentia based on its predicted availability. I also booked lodging in Trinity and two boat trips on separate days to improve my chances. Needless to say, our ferry trip was canceled , and we were rebooked to Port aux Basques.

I canceled that trip, booked the Argentia ferry again for a later date, and changed all the other arrangements after spending two hours on hold before I could speak with a Marine Atlantic agent to schedule the trip. Once again, the voyage was canceled because the ship still wasn't ready to sail. I gave up and scheduled the route to Port aux Basques, departing at 4:30 p.m. on July 2 and arriving in Newfoundland at midnight. Inexplicably, Aura agreed to this plan. I was putting my marriage in jeopardy to see a bird, but not just any bird, and Aura somehow understood.

We disembarked on time from North Sydney after arriving at the terminal two hours before departure, as required. We slept well in our tiny room in Port aux Basques and hit the road across Newfoundland at about 9 a.m. I had been told a day earlier by a Newfie, in my weekly Tuesday fish queue, that "there's nothing to see" on the eight-hour drive to Trinity Bay. On the contrary, the journey was spectacular, with mountains, lakes, rivers, and the possibility of colliding with a moose. These huge herbivores are neither suicidal nor homicidal; they are just trying to find a place with fewer mosquitoes, but many people die every year from collisions with these huge animals.

We were cruising along with an ETA of 5:30 p.m. when we were stopped behind a line of vehicles that stretched beyond our vision. A bridge was under repair, and all eastbound traffic was halted while westbound traffic was allowed to continue. We were stuck for nearly three hours. Aura assisted a motorcyclist who was suffering in the breezeless heat. A good Samaritan passed out popsicles to the waiting travelers. Thus, everyone kept their cool. We never got an explanation for why the eastbound traffic was not allowed to alternate with the westbound traffic. We arrived at our comfortable inn in Trinity just in time to follow the advice of our hostess and go straight to the Dock Marina Café before it closed.

I awoke in the middle of the night with anxiety. I was scheduled to be on the 1 p.m. boat to look for the eagle. I was concerned I might miss the erratic bird once again, so I decided to get to the Eco Tours Lodge early and see if I could get on the 9 a.m. boat to have two chances to find her. There was one space available, so I walked back to the inn to tell Aura my plan. If I saw Stella in the morning, I could give someone my spot in the afternoon and spend some time with Aura in Trinity, a picturesque fishing village with brightly colored houses and well-tended gardens typical of Newfoundland.

My breakfast was included in my tour, so I arrived at the inflated but seaworthy Zodiak with a full belly and guarded optimism. There were two boats, one for birders and the other for whale watchers, but the two skippers were in constant radio contact to optimize everyone's experience. The boat was powered by two 150-horsepower outboard engines that made it very fast. The weather was perfect, and the water was flat. Three hours later, we had seen three species of whales, Atlantic Puffins, Arctic Terns, dozens of Bald Eagles, incredible geographic sights, and several historic coastal villages—but no Steller's Sea Eagle. I returned to Aura with drooping shoulders;

I don't think I had ever coveted a bird as much. The number on my list had nothing to do with it.

An hour later, I was again at sea, this time with a group of birders from western Canada. This trip would be shorter, so we headed straight for the eagle's usual habitat. We cruised the shore in silence, intently studying the cliffs and conifers for the telltale white shoulders that distinguish the Sea Eagle from the numerous Bald Eagles. We were approaching the end of the headlands that protruded into the Bay from the village of Old Bonaventure. This was the last place where Stella had been seen. I must have been cyanotic from holding my breath when the man in front of me silently pointed upward to a tall spruce about a hundred feet up the cliff.

On a bare branch of a towering spruce tree perched a gigantic raptor that displayed a large white mantle around the shoulders.

Mantle: The back of the bird between the neck and the rump; nothing to do with baseball or the New York Yankees.

A closer look revealed the huge orange bill and a bonus, an orange foot with talons grasping the branch where the bird roosted.

Feet: On which a bird walks when not flying and if not sitting and are reliably found at the end of its legs, even though its legs are really its feet. Raptors' feet have talons.

The tail feathers, which appeared to be worn or damaged, were white. The eye, which looked like an orange target with a dark center, gave the creature a fierce expression. This was, without a doubt, my hard-earned Steller's Sea Eagle, life bird 798, no longer a hope, no longer a nemesis, no longer a quest, no longer a recurring dream, no longer inchoate--- the real thing!

Once we spotted Stella, which is what everyone on the boat called the legendary eagle, as if she were a member of the family, we were able to approach slowly and got very close. I took many photos, a few with startling details. I must confess that my view of the Steller's Sea Eagle was blurred by tears. I said the Shehecheyanu, a Hebrew prayer of gratitude, out loud. No one requested or needed a translation.

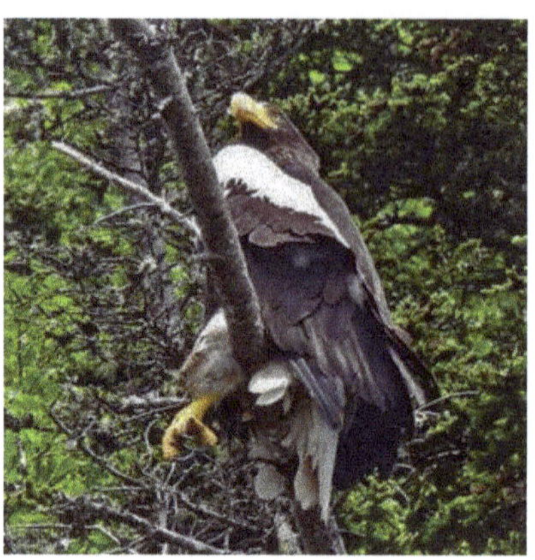

Steller's Sea Eagle
Trinity Bay, Newfoundland

The photographs didn't lie; I was not dreaming or hallucinating. I looked at the images over and over for confirmation. Mick Jagger said, "You can't always get what you want," but sometimes you can, and the reward was worth the effort. As we watched in awe, several Bald Eagles circled Stella and gave their unique clicking sounds. To Stella, the Bald Eagles were nothing more than a nuisance. The Sea Eagle opened its massive beak and uttered a loud grunt of protest but showed no other evidence of stress. She was majestic and in control. She had no mate, but she was not alone.

Later that day, July 4, 2024, Aura and I sat on the porch of a Trinity restaurant, toasting the Steller's Sea Eagle for choosing, like us, to live in Canada. We arrived at the Port aux Basques ferry terminal at 3:30 a.m., two days later, after completing our 1600-kilometre road trip. We managed to get a cabin this time, where we slept in peace for our six-hour crossing. An hour later, our guardian Bald Eagle, Winston, observed our serene return to McNabs Cove, Cape Breton, Canada, from his perch at the top of his favorite ancient yellow birch, where he was in complete control.

THE WILD GOOSE CHASE OF A LIFETIME
LIFE BIRDS 799 AND 800

It was now January 2025. I had been ill for the last five weeks with a mysterious and relentless respiratory virus. My daughter, Jen, had a similar infection that forced her to cancel our reunion at the Algonquin Resort before Christmas in St. Andrews, New Brunswick. In January, I made plans to visit her at her home in Plymouth, MA and have various healthcare appointments. I was not fully recovered and continued with coughing spells that could raise the dead—and make them wish they were still dead.

But I was determined to go.

I had a smooth drive and arrived at the Algonquin, which is exactly half the distance to Plymouth, in mid-afternoon. I arrived in Plymouth in time for the evening meal the next day. I attended my various medical appointments and shared my grief over the death of my first wife's sister, Mary Ann "Mac" Perks. She had been a sister to me, even though I had little contact with her after my marriage to Irene ended in 1984. She and her husband, Will, lived in a refuge in the primal forest of the Catskill Mountains, where they both taught in the Saugerties, New York, public school system. They had three children and six grandchildren. Before they married, they attended the legendary Woodstock Music Festival in 1969 and never tired of talking about it.

It is my custom to check the ABA Rare Bird alert daily, and I was astonished to discover that two species of Bean Goose, Taiga and Tundra, were being reported respectively from the area near Saratoga, New York, along the Hudson River and from a high school ball field in Portsmouth, Rhode Island. These were both within driving distance. Jen decided to accompany me on the three-hour trip to New York for the Taiga Bean Goose. We would search for the goose, spend the night in Saratoga, visit my former nurse practitioner Megan and her husband Ken for breakfast, then return to Plymouth. Megan was invaluable as my assistant during my years as Chief of Pediatric Hematology-Oncology at Albany Medical College from 1982 to 1988. Ken is a pediatrician who was one of my students during my last two years in Albany.

We departed on Saturday after breakfast and soon found ourselves on the iconic Massachusetts Pike that passes through the Berkshire Mountains between Boston and Albany. The scenic highway passes Worcester, MA, where I rowed as a college student, Stockbridge, where I had visited the Norman Rockwell Museum, and the college towns of Holyoke, Northampton, and Williamstown, where some of the prestigious New England Colleges are located. We also passed Amherst, MA, home of Amherst College and poet Emily Dickinson, one of my favorites. Snow flurries provided the perfect setting for us to listen to James Taylor's soothing lullaby, Sweet Baby James, as we traveled the same wintry highway. We shared other music that helped us mourn Jen's aunt, my sister-in-law, and shed a few therapeutic tears together.

We reached the New York Thruway and headed north until our GPS directed us to drive east toward the Hudson River. We reached the Hudson in the village of Watervliet, where I often went to eat cheap pizza and drink Genesee Cream Ale in my days of relative poverty when I first joined the faculty of Albany Medical College. We passed through several other villages haunted by the ghosts of Aaron Burr and Alexander Hamilton. It was as if we had traveled back in time as we passed Victorian mansions and other buildings from centuries past.

We arrived at Hudson Crossing in the town of Schuylerville around noon, the site of the most recent reports of our goose. This is a picturesque spot on the Hudson River north of Albany and east of Saratoga Springs. We were greeted by a lovely young couple, thrilled novice birders who had seen and photographed the Taiga Bean Goose. They told us that the goose had just flown south. We decided to wait for its return and managed to join a group on the social media site Discord, which would provide us with real-time updates and the chance to communicate with other goosers.

The goose did not return to Hudson Crossing, but eventually was spotted with hundreds of Canada geese in some cornfields a few miles north in the township of Greenwich. We charged to that site, but missed the bird and visited other hot spots along the Hudson with no luck. Finally, as dusk approached, we got another report that the bird was spotted in the same cornfields but farther east. We arrived in time to get a brief look at the goose in fading light and cold rain. It could

Taiga Bean Goose, Life Bird 799
Note the Mostly Orange Broad Bill and White Streaks

be distinguished from the Canada Geese by its lighter grey back with distinct white linear markings. Once in a while, it would lift its head to display its orange bill. My photo attempts were corrupted by poor light, but we could see the back of the goose. Despite the poor view, this was life bird 799: Only one bird left to make 800 lifers!

We drove to our hotel in Saratoga and went out for dinner. The restaurant was directly across the street from the famous Hattie's Chicken Shack, a Saratoga landmark for a century. Hattie's is famous for its Southern fried chicken and honey-encrusted French toast. After we ate, we bought a container of Ben and Jerry's ice cream and returned to our cozy room, where we ate the ice cream and watched some mindless television. For some reason, I couldn't fall asleep.

Jen, although not a certified birder, has the determination of one. She insisted that we return to our goose's domain at dawn to get a better look before driving to Albany to see Megan and Ken. I obeyed my intransigent daughter, and we visited several likely sites without finding the goose. (It was reported a few hours later from one of those sites.) We made our way to Albany and had waffles and coffee with the Kroopniks. We bought an assortment of bagels for them, which Ken rejected as they were not Kosher. Megan had a huge grin on her face when we arrived. She and I had survived numerous intense experiences together and never lost our mutual respect and affection. We had a long hug which was enabled by being with my daughter and not my wife. We spent about two hours with our hosts, then returned to Plymouth.

We truly enjoyed our journey. Jen loved being part of the camaraderie that birders enjoy, especially when a rare bird is being pursued. The Taiga Bean Goose had never been seen in New York, and Jen's technical prowess was instrumental in finally getting a look. Without her, I'm sure I wouldn't have seen the bird. She had helped bring me to the precipice of my quest.

Once back in Plymouth, I confirmed the Tundra Bean Goose was still being seen daily in the afternoon at Portsmouth High School in Newport, R.I., a 55-minute drive from Jen's house. I decided to go and give it a try. If found, it would be Life Bird number 800. The probability of finding two species of rare geese within driving distance is diminishingly small, but I had the opportunity. Accordingly, I drove to Newport to arrive early and wait for the geese to arrive at the school. When I arrived, several other cars were there for the same reason. It got to be 4:00 p.m., and the birds hadn't arrived. I checked my eBird rare bird alert and noted that the goose had been found about 10 minutes away in a cornfield. I rushed to the site and arrived at 4:20, four minutes after the goose flew away.

I returned to Plymouth, certain that I had blown my chances for this rare goose and my 800th life bird. The next morning, I noticed that the goose had been reported at 6:45 a.m. at Lawton Valley Reservoir, just minutes from the cornfield where it was seen the day before. The observer correctly concluded that he had discovered where the Bean Goose, along with about two hundred of its Canadian comrades, spent each night in a small area of open water. Armed with this new information, I decided to try again. In retrospect, our efforts to find the Taiga Bean Goose had been hampered by the Hudson River, where the goose and its allies might spend the night at multiple locations instead of just one, like the Tundra Bean Goose.

Tundra Bean Goose, Life Bird 800
Note the Ruddy Brown Head, White Streaks,
and Orange Tip of the Slender Bill

I drove to the cornfield and also checked the school. There were many birders in the area, and I exchanged contact information so we could let one another know if the goose was found. By about 4:00 p.m., the bird had not been found, although a large flock of geese landed briefly in the cornfield, but appeared to be spooked by all the cars and left before we could carefully look for it. Subsequently, a single Canada goose flew over the site and then disappeared. I believe this bird was a scout dispatched to check the area and decided that there were too many humans there. I have not been able to determine if this behavior has been observed and/or corroborated by others.

I decided to end my day at the reservoir that I checked earlier when all the geese were out foraging, God knows where. I parked my truck and started to walk on the dike to the open water where the geese would spend the night. I noticed a flock of birders with scopes on a hill beyond the open water. This was my best chance. I hustled back to the truck to join the group. As I did so, I noticed a huge flock of geese squawking their way back to their roosting area.

By the time I reached my fellow wild goose chasers, one of them, a lady in her twenties, had her scope focused on the Tundra Bean Goose. She showed it to me and many others and helped everyone locate the bird, which was difficult to find in the fading light as it swam constantly among the innumerable Canada geese. The goose had its head tucked and only occasionally showed its narrow bill with the telltale orange band around it. Once I got a good look, thanks to my new colleague, I felt the electric enormity of what had just happened.

I had just seen Life Bird 800.

I had a grin on my face large enough to display my crowned molars. The young woman looked at my jack-o-lantern grin and gave me a silent look of inquiry.

"Eight hundred," I stammered.

She announced my achievement to the many nearby birders. They offered a brief round of muted applause to avoid spooking the bird. One had made the journey from Alberta to chase this goose. No words were necessary; they understood.

I was stunned, I was elated—and I was exhausted.

I returned to Jen's house in Plymouth to share a warm meal, music by the fire, and my 800th life bird with family.

What could be better?

REFLECTIONS

I have been a passionate birder for fifty years. I have traveled more than 100,000 miles and visited innumerable places in search of birds that I surely wouldn't have seen otherwise. I have spent thousands of dollars and challenged relationships and my livelihood. I accomplished my goal of seeing 800 species of birds in North America.

When I look back on all this, what do I see?

First, and most importantly, I have grown as a person. I see the world not simply as a playground for humans, but a delicate and fragile miracle of complexity and beauty that is in deep peril. As a human living in this challenging world, I have gained humility: The more you learn about nature and birds, the more you know how insignificant you are, and how fortunate you are to spend some part of your allotted time observing the triumphant glory of planet earth and its inhabitants. Humility is something we all sorely need, and I offer these moments of wonder—with my simple "rules" for birding and living discovered along the way—in hopes that they might help you find a little more of it too.

I began by asking why I and many others are passionate enough about birding to sacrifice so much in pursuit of our avian quarry, often neglecting other responsibilities. While I can't give you a simple answer, because there is none, I can say that the answer is a puzzle, and this book contains many of its pieces.

Birding provides a means of escape from the "sound and fury" of daily life to the natural world where, with a little effort and even less skill, a person can find beauty and tranquility whenever it is needed. For me, these nexuses with the natural world are a source of spirituality, a sense that you are part of something bigger than yourself or any of your personal issues. The direct identification of a bird with its shape, its color, its characteristic "field marks" that distinguish it from all other species, is a portal for me to get as close as I can to what others find through faith. These moments are an affirmation that life, with all its sadness and the certainty of death, is a place where anybody can access spectacular beauty and find moments of absolute joy and serenity.

Then there are the birds themselves. I have seen all of the indigenous nesting birds between the Mexican border and the North American Arctic. Each is the outcome of millions of years of evolution. Some are found daily in the yard, others require traveling to the most remote corners of the continent, but each is uniquely perfect. Painting these many birds over the years has drawn me considerably closer to the staggering detail unique to each one, and the rarities and introduced species add another level of exhilaration that goes beyond the birds that have been here since the aftermath of the dinosaurs.

Birding can be a solitary activity. There is poetry in the notion of being alone in the natural world where you can observe with minimal impact. I, however, like most people, need other people with whom to share my life experiences. I learned, in retrospect, that I had not taken my relationships with others as seriously as I should have and suffered losses as a result, including two divorces and four children with broken families. I grew to realize that my birding needed to be shared to be fully experienced. I learned to take pleasure in sharing my birding successes with others and to appreciate those who assisted me in my endeavors. I endured danger, cold, crippling fatigue, and any number of other misfortunes to be with others who shared my love of birds and birding. This knowledge did not come easily for me, a natural loner, but birding was my ticket to a wider life of human interaction and shared adventures.

What about the quest for 800 birds? I resolved late in my life to challenge myself to achieve something in birding that few others can claim. This required dragging my ancient body on arduous journeys, which challenged all my faculties and subjected me to the humiliating reality that I am a member of an older generation that is uncomfortable with the new age of technology.

I was successful in reaching my elusive goal, but I also learned in the process that much of what I had enjoyed so much about birding was corrupted by this ardent pursuit. The birds that are the stars of the show, not me or how many I have seen. But because of what it has taught me, I don't regret my decision. My Latin teacher from high school challenged me to be a lifelong scholar, and I think I met the challenge.

EPILOGUE

When I took up birding during my pediatric training, I had no idea where it would lead. When I began writing down my experiences, I hoped the process would give me a greater understanding of my passion for birding and, in due course, myself.

I believe my hopes have been realized. In this context, seeing 800 species provided the rails, but the train was me.

This testimony of my many and diverse experiences as a birder of limited skill but high motivation serves as an autobiography of sorts, beginning in my twenties. It represents, as discussed previously, a counterpoint to my life as a physician, husband, and parent. Birding freed my artistic right brain and made me a more complete person. I have faced some health challenges since I began this project, but I have reason to believe that I will have many more experiences worth relating.

Of course, at age 80, one never knows. Thus, this story does not come to an end—until it ends.

Appendix 1

THE BIRDHOUSE RULES

RULE 1   If you have goals worth pursuing, persist no matter what, and you will be rewarded in kind. (Although I cannot predict what kind.)

RULE 2   Never begin a book with a glossary or definition. (You might sound pedantic.)

RULE 3   Pride is a paralytic poison that kills relationships.

RULE 4   Give people *dan le-khat zekhut* (benefit of the doubt) even if they talk funny, were enemies in the Civil War, and use words like onest or twicet.

RULE 5   When opportunities present themselves, seize them.

RULE 6   Anyone can make a difference, and any difference matters.

RULE 7   Don't let a day pass without experiencing beauty.

RULE 8   Not everything has an explanation, so accept the good and bad as part of life, which itself has no explanation.

RULE 9   Individual goals are seldom accomplished without the assistance of others.

RULE 10   No fence is strong enough or high enough to withstand human kindness.

RULE 11   Teachers should be the most valued of all people.

RULE 12   Many pleasurable things come with pain, but don't let the pain prevent the pleasure.

RULE 13   Nothing is perfect, but some imperfections are preventable.

RULE 14   Aging is a challenge accelerated by passivity.

RULE 15   Any creative behavior is likely to be met with suspicion, especially if it involves crossing borders or your neighbor's driveway.

RULE 16   In birding, as in everything else, family comes first, for the birder and the birds.

RULE 17   If nature were our judge and jury, we would face a harsh verdict.

RULE 18   When all is dark, listen.

RULE 19   Our upright posture separates us from the apes, so for Darwin's sake, stand up and walk.

RULE 20   If you are Jewish and find yourself in a place where you must eat fresh crab and lobster, don't tell the rabbi.

RULE 21   Our upright posture separates us from the apes, so for Darwin's sake, and your own, keep on walking.

RULE 22   If you see a penguin north of the equator, consult your eye doctor and/or your psychiatrist; if the bird is not a hallucination, it is most likely a puffin.

RULE 23   In Alaska, if you go too far, you may never come back.

RULE 24   A frustrating irony is to search for something in futility, then find it when you are not looking for it. (But if you expect to find things by not looking for them, you are throwing moss at a glass house.)

RULE 25   If you find yourself zig-zagging through an Oklahoma prairie, either you're caught in a tornado or you're in an Oklahoma birder's SUV.

RULE 26   There is much to be learned from the young if you are not.

| **RULE 27** | Aversion to risk carries the risk of squandering benefits. |

| **RULE 28** | Once you commit to a challenging goal, be ready to embrace the inevitable failure that amplifies the success. Both will stay with you as long as you live, and we all need company. |

| **RULE 29** | Spending time alone in a chilly graveyard waiting in futility for a bird to appear has nothing to do with the subsequent discovery of the bird somewhere else, but it should. |

| **RULE 30** | You can't go home again. |

| **RULE 31** | One rare bird found is worth at least two missed. |

| **RULE 32** | Catching a glimpse of a rare flycatcher is impressive and better than catching a glimpse of just any flycatcher, especially with this catchy repetition. |

| **RULE 33** | You can go home again. |

| **RULE 34** | With few exceptions, no goal is unobtainable until you decide it is. |

| **RULE 35** | While the day is fast approaching when we will not know if we are dealing with a human or a bot, wild birds are the real thing. |

| **RULE 36** | Making mistakes is good practice for getting it right. |

| **RULE 37** | Dreams can come true, and the truth can be as good as the dream. |

| **RULE 38** | If you start climbing, you might reach the top. |

Appendix 2

A BIRDERS' GLOSSARY

GENERAL TERMS

Accidental: A species found where it is not expected to be, also called a vagrant. This phenomenon also occurs in humans, often with unfortunate consequences.

Bird: A vertebrate that is not an amphibian, a reptile, a fish, or a mammal; all have feathers, and most have wings and can fly, while a few hapless species have grown flippers instead of wings and spend a good deal of their time on the ground where they are likely to be eaten, shot, or run over by a birder.

Birder: Term used to describe anyone who goes out to look for birds; however, there are many levels of birderdom, and there is a stereotype (that is often not so stereotypical,) of the typical birder. This stereotype includes drab and formless clothing, functional to outlandish hats, vests and backpacks to carry variable amounts of field guides, binoculars, cameras, and all manner of unnecessary paraphernalia. Birders tend toward eccentric behavior and the wearing of patches to let the world know where they have been, as if anyone cared. It is not true that all birders are lunatics, but many are. One thing we must clarify is that birders seldom "watch" birds, and the term birdwatcher is not only inaccurate but pejorative. Although there are times when more prolonged observation is required for identification or desirable because of a particular behavior, lingering too long while "watching" one bird is likely to result in not seeing other birds or oncoming vehicles driven by birders.

Call: Sounds made by birds that are not songs but could come from a bird that can sing if it wants to, or from one that cannot. Birds call when they please, not to please birders.

Countable: An introduced bird that can be added to the birder's list if seen in a place where it breeds, The choice of locations like Texas and Miami should not be held against the birds that were clever enough to escape from human captors who brought them there without their permission.

Dihedral: The geometry of a flying bird whose wings are held higher than the horizontal while soaring; this is nothing of which the bird should be ashamed but is typical of vultures.

GISS: A term that sounds worse than it is. It was probably derived from airplane identification during World War II in which the letters stood for General Impression of Size and Shape. In birding, the term more broadly means the impression that a bird gives of size, shape, behavior, flight, etc., which allows identification without being able to study the bird more carefully, or shooting it, which, despite Audubon, is generally frowned upon, especially by carrier pigeons, if they weren't extinct and if they could frown.

Lifer: A species of bird seen for the first time in a birder's life, not necessarily the bird's life. This is an iconic event for birders and of such great importance that it can challenge the judgement (and honesty), of any birder. Thus photography (un-doctored), which I took up late in my career as a birder, is arguably the surest way to be certain that a bird has been seen. As with much of life, there is no absolute certainty, especially with the odd birder (redundancy) who is afflicted with voluntary hallucinations.

Lister: Nothing to do with mouthwash, someone who keeps a list or lists of birds seen. This can range from one's backyard, bathtub, state or province, country, or the world. This term can be used in a derogatory way to describe birders who are less interested in the birds than in the list(s). Often lists are carried to an extreme: for example, birds seen on Mondays perched on electrical wires when the observer is wearing wingtip shoes and a floppy fedora.

Owling: The name given to the practice of benighted birders who venture out on a dark night, usually in February or March, when owls are most vocal, in hopes of finding and/or counting owls who can see in the dark whilst birders cannot.

Pishing: a noise like running water made by birders to attract birds, which annoys and alarms most non-birders enough to keep them away.

Song: That which may be heard when a bird sings if it is a bird that can sing and chooses to do so.

Twitch: This describes the behavior, more or less unique to birders, of dropping everything at a moment's notice to dash off to see birds. An extreme example of this is a neurosurgeon at my hospital who left his post to chase a bird without arranging for anyone to cover his patients and lost his license as a result. Other forms of twitching are not relevant to this book but are certainly important to those who are doing the twitching.

Twitcher: A birder who takes twitching to an extreme, which earns him or her this dubious description and often results in calamitous effects on earnings, relationships, and country club memberships, but does result in an impressive list of birds.

Vagrant: Also called an accidental which presumes that the bird has no reason to be where it is. Owners of parrots should teach their pets to recite their address if asked by a birder.

ANATOMICAL TERMS

Auriculars: Areas on both sides of the head where the ears would be if birds had ears. Birds do not have ears, unlike rabbits and elephants, but sometimes do have colorful spots instead.

Beak (bill): That part of the bird that extends from the head in front of the eyes and is used to crack seeds, catch prey, obtain fluids, and build nests. It is also used appropriately to bite or peck feckless people who handle birds without their permission.

Belly: The underside of a bird that resembles the protuberant equivalent of some people who have consumed too much beer and eaten too many pork rinds. In the case of birds, the belly is likely to be gracefully curved and decorated with colorful feathers.

Collar: The part of a bird below the head where a collar might be if birds wore shirts. Birds seldom dress up, and I would give the shirt off my back if someone could think of a better name.

Coverts: The feathers above and below the base of the tail; nothing to do with espionage; birders are more likely to be spies than birds are, and sometimes use birding as an excuse for window peeping.

Crown (cap): That part of a bird from which a tuft extends if the bird has a tuft or where the bird sports a kippah if Jewish, a sombrero if Mexican, or a beanie if pledged to a fraternity.

Eyes: The parts of a bird with which the bird sees and that are located on the sides of the head, which is not true of humans unless they have had excessive plastic surgery.

Feathers: Feathery skin appendages that are a requirement for all birds, but there are all different kinds of feathers (e.g., primary, secondary, scapulars, etc.), which might be of interest to some birders, but not to me or the birds; also, something often worn on the heads of people who are inexplicably trying to look like birds, which is especially hazardous behavior during pheasant -hunting season.

Feet: On which a bird walks when not flying if not sitting and are reliably found at the end of its legs, even though its legs are really its feet. Raptors feet have talons.

Flanks: The sides of a bird above the belly that usually cannot be distinguished from the belly unless someone has written the word "flank" on both sides of the bird in the appropriate location, something that I have never observed. Some birds have stripes or dots on their flanks, so labelling them is not necessary.

Gape: The fleshy tissue behind the bill of some birds, especially gulls, which, when they open their bills to squawk, makes them look like they just ate a hot dog with mustard and ketchup; in the case of gulls, this is entirely possible.

Head: This speaks for itself.

Legs: With which a bird walks and to which are attached the feet, which, in the case of raptors, have talons used to catch prey. Some birds are named after their legs, which people are not, e.g., Yellow-legged Gull or Rough-legged Hawk. Can you imagine someone being called a Red-legged Michigander?

Lores: The part of the face in front of the eyes, and that may give the impression of spectacles, which birds don't commonly wear, since their eyes are on the sides of their heads, except for owls which wisely avoid spectacles.

Mandible: The lower part of the bill which is found directly below the upper bill (maxilla). Together, these form the pecker with which a bird, if it is a pecker, pecks.

Mantle: The back of the bird between the neck and the rump; nothing to do with baseball or the New York Yankees.

Mustache: Some birds are described as having mustaches. This is fine for the males, but can be confusing to the females.

Nape: The area between the mantle and the head, assuming the bird has both.

Rump: The part of the bird from which the tail extends and that is yellow in the case of the Yellow-rumped Warbler.

Supercilium: The part of the bird's face above the eye that can make certain birds appear to be supercilious although this is unlikely, unless they are "encaged" in a "bored" meeting on Zoom.

Tail: Extends south from the rump when the bird is flying north.

Tarsus: The lower leg of a bird, which points forward instead of backward because it is a foot and the foot is the toes which is very confusing to podiatrists, some of whom have exclaimed, "Foot, my foot, but it still needs bunion surgery!"

Toes: Of which most birds have four, three forward, and one backward, although I have never seen a bird walking backward.

Tuft: A silly triangular point of feathers on the crown of some birds that resembles some unfortunate hairdo choices that I often refer to as hair don'ts.

Whiskers: Hairlike feathers that project from the base of the bill and are used to detect edible insects and avoid inedible things like fingers.

Wings: Without these, it cannot be a bird and cannot fly, although there are flightless birds whose wings have evolved into fins (penguins), or if you are a Creationist, were created defectively on the Fifth Day as Moses was crossing the Delaware.

Appendix 3

A BIRDERS' GLOSSARY

THE BIRDS
Listed in alphabetical order (does not include all 800 life birds).

Acadian Flycatcher
Aleutian Tern
Altamira Oriole
American Woodcock (771)
Ancient Murrelet
Antillean Nighthawk
Aplomado Falcon (780)
Arctic Loon
Arctic Warbler
Atlantic Puffin
Audubon's Oriole
Bachmann's Sparrow
Baird's Sparrow
Bald Eagle
Bare-throated Tiger Heron (792)
Barnacle Goose
Barnacle Goose (777)
Barred Owl
Bar-tailed Godwit
Bat Falcon
Bicknell's Thrush
Bicknell's Thrush (798)
Black Noddy
Black Rail
Black Rosy Finch
Black-billed Cuckoo
Black-footed Albatross
Black-legged Kittiwake
Black-tailed Godwit
Black-tailed Gull
Blue Bunting
Bluethroat
Bobwhite Quail
Boreal Chickadee
Botteri's Sparrow
Bridled Tern
Bristle-thighed Curlew
Bronzed Cowbird
Brown Booby
Brown Noddy
Brown-capped Rosy Finch
Brown-headed Cowbird
Buff-breasted Sandpiper
Buff-collared Nightjar
California Condor
Canada Warbler (772)
Carolina Wren
Cerulean Warbler
Chestnut-collared Longspur
Chuck-will's-widow
Clay-colored Robin
Colima Warbler
Common Murre
Common Pauraque
Common Shelduck (791)
Connecticut Warbler
Couch's Kingbird
Crested Auklet
Crested Caracara
Curlew Sandpiper
Dark-eyed Junco
Dovekie

Little Egret (776)
Little Gull
Dunlin
Dusky Grouse
Dusky Grouse
Eastern Whip-poor-will
Elegant Trogon
Elf Owl
Emperor Goose
Eurasian Hobby
Eurasian Skylark
European Golden Plover
Fan-tailed Warbler (795)
Ferruginous Pygmy Owl
Fieldfare
Five-striped Sparrow
Flame-coloured Tanager
Florida Scrub Jay
Fork-tailed Flycatcher (767)
Fork-tailed Storm-Petrel (765)
Golden Eagle
Golden-crowned Warbler (779)
Grace's Warbler
Gray Partridge
Gray Vireo
Gray-collared Becard (794)
Gray-crowned Rosy Finch
Great Black Hawk
Great-crested Flycatcher
Great Gray Owl
Great Kiskadee
Greater Prairie Chicken
Greater Sage Grouse
Green Jay
Green Parakeet
Grey Hawk
Grey Heron (775)
Grey Kingbird
Groove-billed Ani
Gunnison Sage Grouse
Gyrfalcon
Harlequin Duck
Harris's Hawk
Henslow's Sparrow
Hoary Redpoll
Hooded Oriole
Hooded Warbler
Hook-billed Kite (782)
Horned Lark
Horned Puffin
Ivory Gull
Kentucky Warbler
King Eider
Kirtland's Warbler
Kittlitz's Murrelet (790)
Lapland Longspur
LaSagra's Flycatcher
Laysan Albatross
Least Auklet
Least Bittern
LeConte's Sparrow
Lesser Prairie Chicken

Limpkin
Long-tailed Duck
Long-tailed Jaeger
Lucifer Hummingbird
Lucy's Warbler
Mangrove Cuckoo
Manx Shearwater (785)
Marbled Murrelet
Masked Booby
Masked Duck
McKay's Bunting
Mexican Whip-poor-will
Montezuma Quail
Mottled Owl (796)
Mountain Quail
Mourning Warbler
Nanday Parakeet
Nelson's Sparrow (774)
Northern Cardinal
Northern Flicker
Northern Fulmar
Northern Hawk Owl
Northern Lapwing (778)
Northern Mockingbird
Northern Saw-whet Owl
Nutting's Flycatcher
Nutting's Flycatcher (784)
Pacific Wren
Painted Bunting
Painted Redstart
Parakeet Auklet
Pectoral Sandpiper
Peregrine Falcon
Pileated Woodpecker
Pine Flycatcher
Pine Warbler
Pink-footed Goose (766)
Plain Chachalaca
Prothonotary Warbler
Purple Sandpiper
Purple Sandpiper
Red Crossbill
Red-billed Tropicbird
Red-cockaded Woodpecker
Red-cockaded Woodpecker
Red-crowned Parrot
Red-faced Cormorant
Red-footed Falcon
Red-legged Kittiwake
Red-necked Grebe
Red-necked Stint (786)
Redwing
Resplendent Quetzal
Rhinoceros Auklet
Ridgway's Rail (783)
Roadside Hawk
Roadside Hawk (792)
Rock Ptarmigan
Rock Sandpiper
Rock Sandpiper
Roseate Tern
Rose-throated Becard

Ross's Gull
Ruff
Rufous-backed Robin (768)
Rufous-crowned Warbler
Rufous-winged Sparrow
Sabine's Gull
Saltmarsh Sparrow
Scissor-tailed Flycatcher
Seaside Sparrow
Sharp-tailed Sandpiper
Short-tailed Shearwater (789)
Siberian Accentor
Silky Cowbird
Slate-throated Redstart
Smith's Longspur
Smooth-billed Ani
Snail Kite
Snow Bunting
Snow Goose
Social Flycatcher (781)
Sooty Grouse
Sooty Tern
Spectacled Eider (787)
Spotted Owl
Sprague's Pipit
Spruce Grouse
Steller's Eider
Steller's Sea Eagle (797)
Summer Tanager
Swainson's Warbler
Taiga Bean Goose (799)
Thick-billed Kingbird
Thick-billed Longspur
Thick-billed Murre
Tropical Kingbird
Tufted Duck
Tufted Flycatcher
Tufted Puffin
Tundra Bean Goose (800)
Varied Bunting
Veery (773)
Vermilion Flycatcher
Whiskered Auklet
Whiskered Auklet (788)
Whiskered Screech Owl
Whiskered Screech Owl
White-eyed Parakeet
White-headed Woodpecker
White-tailed Hawk
White-tailed Ptarmigan
White-winged Parakeet
Whooping Crane
Willow Flycatcher
Willow Ptarmigan
Wilson's Plover
Yellow Rail
Yellow-bellied Flycatcher
Yellow-billed Cuckoo
Yellow-rumped Warbler
Yellow-throated Warbler
Zone-tailed Hawk

ACKNOWLEDGMENTS

I would like to acknowledge all those who taught me about birds and birding, especially Dr. Michael Linshaw, Arnold Small, Larry Manfredi, Melody Kehl, and Steven McGrath. I also want to credit my Latin teacher, Ethyl B. Sager, for convincing me to "learn something about everything and everything about something." I want to thank my esteemed editor, James Bock, for guiding me through "good trouble" and my team captain Thomas Hurd and his superb design collaborator, creative director Madeline Mafilios, for transforming a book into a work of art.

Dr. Edward Arenson is a retired oncologist and neuro-oncologist. He was born in Philadelphia, PA and grew up in Toledo, Ohio, where he has been honored for lifetime achievements. He attended Cornell University, majoring in English literature and specializing in early American writing. Dr. Arenson attended medical school at Drexel University and specialized in childhood cancer. He lives in Cape Breton, Nova Scotia, Canada, with his wife, Aura.

Photo by Katy Tartakoff